Easy Home Improvements

Julian Cassell
Peter Parham

TIME
LIFE
BOOKS

Alexandria, Virginia

TIME LIFE INC.
President and CEO Jim Nelson

TIME-LIFE TRADE PUBLISHING
Vice President and Publisher Neil Levin
Senior Director of Acquisitions and Editorial
Resources Jennifer Pearce
Director of New Product Development
Carolyn Clark
Director of Trade Sales Dana Coleman
Director of Marketing Inger Forland
Director of New Product Development
Teresa Graham
Director of Custom Publishing John Lalor
Director of Special Markets Robert Lombardi
Director of Design Kate L. McConnell
Project Manager Jennie Halfant

Originated in Singapore by Chroma Graphics.
Printed and bound in China by Excel Printing.
10 9 8 7 6 5 4 3 2 1

TIME-LIFE is a trademark of Time Warner Inc.,
and affiliated companies.

Front cover photography: **John Freeman** (top and
centre) **Elizabeth Whiting and Associates** (bottom
left) **Tim Ridley** (bottom centre) **Nick Huggins/
Houses & Interiors** (bottom left)
Back cover photography: **Tim Ridley**

Library of Congress Cataloging-in-Publication Data
Cassell, Julian.
Easy home improvements: the essential guide to home
decorating / Julian Cassell & Peter Parham.
p. cm. — (Time-Life do-it-yourself factfile)
Includes index
ISBN: 0-7370-0311-1 (spiral bound: alk. paper)
1. Dwellings—Remodeling—Amateurs' manuals.
2. Interior decoration—Amateurs' manuals. I. Parham,
Peter. II. Title. III. Series.

TH4816.C33 2000
643'.7—dc21   99-089111

Books produced by Time-Life Trade Publishing are
available at a special bulk discount for promotional
and premium use. Custom adaptations can also be
created to meet your specific marketing goals.
Call 1-800-323-5255.

Marshall Editions
Project Editor Felicity Jackson

Designed by Martin Lovelock & John Round

Photographer Tim Ridley

Illustrations Chris Forsey

Managing Art Editor Patrick Carpenter

Managing Editor Antonia Cunningham

Editorial Director Ellen Dupont

Art Director Dave Goodman

Editorial Coordinator Ros Highstead

Production Nikki Ingram

Indexer Hilary Bird

Note

Every effort has been taken to ensure that all information in this book is correct and compatible with
national standards generally accepted at the time of publication. This book is not intended to replace
manufacturer's instructions in the use of their tools and materials—always follow their safety guidelines.
The author and publisher disclaim any liability, loss, injury or damage incurred as a consequence, directly
or indirectly, of the use and application of the contents of this book.

CONTENTS

INTRODUCTION

F rom time to time we all look at different rooms in our homes and decide that it is time to make a few changes to improve their appearance and generally remodel and refurbish them to keep pace with fashion, style, and changes in personal taste. This process can be carried out on a large scale with a complete overhaul of the room, or it can be a matter of adding a few details here and there to give a new look. This book covers a range of remodeling ideas—large and small—and provides the technical know-how, illustrated with clear step-by-step instructions, to help you make all manner of home improvements. Never before have manufacturers offered so many materials and tools all aimed at producing particular styles and looks in the home—the choice of finishes and effects has never been greater. Much of the fun of improving your home is in the decision-making process, combining your ideas with professional advice on how best to produce results that will be beneficial to the look of your home and very rewarding in terms of personal achievement.

BUDGETING FOR A REVAMP

The main concern with any home improvement is to decide on its extent and how much time and money you are prepared to commit to the job. The personal pleasure you will get from a new look should be balanced against such facts as whether you intend to stay in the house for a long time, or if you plan to move in the near future and will therefore only get a short-term return. However, while it is nice to be able to enjoy the fruits of your labor for as long as possible, remember that any home improvement will usually add to the value of your home. This is one good reason to go into any remodeling job with the attitude that you want to produce the best possible finish, regardless of whether you intend to stay in the house for a long time or plan to move shortly—the result of your work will be beneficial one way or another.

ESSENTIAL FIXTURES

All homes have a selection of fixtures that fulfill relatively straightforward functions but are essential for the smooth running of the household. Despite the fact that these fixtures can carry out very simple functions, there is a wide choice of styles to choose from. Chapter 1 covers all the essential aspects of this important area of any refurbishment project, guiding you through the choices, advising on personal needs, and demonstrating how systems may be installed in the home.

PRODUCING A STYLE

Once the essential fixtures in the home have been improved, you can turn your attention to the more creative task of adding style to the rooms. Chapter 2 illustrates many ways in which it is possible to add character to existing schemes. All the techniques in this chapter aim to take the basic shell of a room and achieve a different look by adding various embellishments to the walls, ceilings, or woodwork.

RENOVATING FLOORS

Try to keep in touch with modern developments, as the choice and variety of floorcoverings are constantly increasing. This area of refurbishment has become much more accessible to the home decorator since manufacturers have made it easy to lay all kinds of floorcoverings. Chapter 3 provides a whole range of flooring choices, demonstrating how they can be laid to the best possible effect and the best techniques for doing this.

EFFECTIVE STORAGE

Improving or adding to storage areas is an essential part of refurbishment since it can completely transform the general functioning of the household and improve its overall look at the same time. Chapter 4 explores this exciting area of home improvement with lots of good ideas for turning wasted space into storage areas and innovative suggestions for storage systems in general. It explains the principles behind creating storage areas and demonstrates how you can adjust them to your particular needs in your own home.

FINISHING OFF

The finishing touches of home improvement contribute a great deal to the final look and play an essential role in the whole remodeling process. Chapter 5 covers all kinds of finishing ideas, demonstrating the best techniques for adding a variety of features, such as pictures, mirrors, and lights. While many of the items are practical, there are lots of innovative ideas for combining practicality with a highly attractive overall finish.

DEALING WITH PRIORITIES

Home improvements can include so many areas in the home that there needs to be some sort of priority list, otherwise the whole process can become very confused and complicated. This book deals with essential fixtures first and then progresses on to the other areas of concern in the house. After dealing with the essentials, it is always best to turn your attention to the most lived-in areas of the home, since these are the places where you will spend time and gain most benefit from the improvements you make. As a rule, always try to finish one job or project before beginning the next, otherwise there is a danger of the whole house turning into a building site, which can be demoralizing, and take all the enjoyment out of the home improvement process. Above all, remember that the hard work that you put into any revamp will benefit the overall look of your home. Use this book as a source of inspiration as well as an instructional guide in your aim to achieve these personal goals.

QUICK FIXES

Chapter 6 acts as a directory that demonstrates the quickest and most effective ways of carrying out many of the household repairs and maintenance tasks that can be applied to one or more areas in the home, depending on your particular needs. It also has ideas for quick but effective home improvements plus advice on remodeling and decorating specific features in the home rather than entire rooms. Finally, the home safety and maintenance checklists at the end of the chapter will ensure that you always have the systems in your home functioning at optimum level. After all, not every area of home improvement is concerned with looks, and the essential areas of maintenance and safety should always be given very careful attention, so that they can be improved and kept up-to-date with modern developments.

GENERAL TOOLS

I t is impossible to carry out a refurbishment without the appropriate tools for the task. Because this book covers so many areas of home improvement, it is not possible to illustrate every tool you may need. Instead, try to build up a general toolbox that will cover most of the jobs in the home. The tools illustrated here are all useful ones to have.

Hot-air gun

Chisels

Electrical tape

Adjustable wrench

Tape measure

Profile gauge

Workbench

Brick chisel

Sander

Staple gun

Short level

Dust mask

Standard handsaw

Cordless drill/driver

Hacksaw

Jigsaw

Hammer

Plastering float

Stepladder

Miter block

Straight-blade screwdrivers

Cross-head screwdrivers

Plier wrench

DECORATING TOOLS

I n addition to the more general household tools shown on page 9, you will also need some special tools for decorating and for finishing off jobs. Not all the decorating tools shown below will be necessary for all the jobs; you should only buy the tools you need for the particular home improvement project you are planning to carry out. This way, you can gradually build up a decorating toolbox as and when you need the tools.

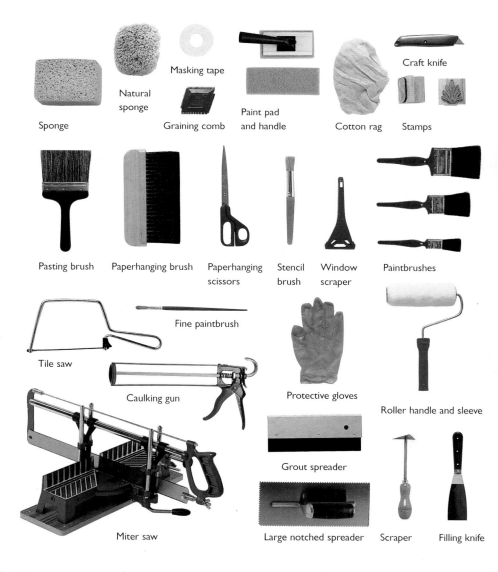

Masking tape

Natural sponge

Sponge

Graining comb

Paint pad and handle

Craft knife

Cotton rag

Stamps

Pasting brush

Paperhanging brush

Paperhanging scissors

Stencil brush

Window scraper

Paintbrushes

Tile saw

Fine paintbrush

Caulking gun

Protective gloves

Roller handle and sleeve

Grout spreader

Miter saw

Large notched spreader

Scraper

Filling knife

Essential Fixtures

Door furniture 12
Choosing and changing your door hardware

Window furniture 14
Selecting and fitting new window hardware

Security fixtures 16
Choosing the correct window and door security for your home

Curtain tracks 18
How to put up a simple curtain or drapery track

Curtain poles 20
The best method for fitting a decorative curtain pole

Double glazing 22
Choosing the best double-glazed windows for your home

Insulating 24
How and where to use insulating materials

Alarms 26
Choosing the best alarm systems to suit your needs

ESSENTIAL
FIXTURES

Certain fixtures are essential for the day-to-day smooth running of the household. This chapter is full of ideas for remodeling and improving them in a style that suits your personal taste and requirements. This chapter also demonstrates the benefits to be gained from carrying out these tasks and explains what is involved, so that you can decide whether the job is one that you want to attempt. It explains the importance of prioritizing areas such as home security and insulation, for example, so that your home is safe and you save on fuel bills. It is important to draw up a plan of your own personal requirements, then you can see what benefits can be gained from these areas of refurbishment.

DOOR FURNITURE

D oor furniture (or hardware) is designed to look good and be practical. Like other fixtures around the home, the cost varies according to the quality. However, one very quick and easy way of updating the appearance of a door is to simply replace the handles.

CHOOSING A STYLE OF DOOR HARDWARE

There is a vast selection of door hardware available, which makes choosing a style quite difficult. However, the choice is narrowed down by the type of doors you have in your home and the handle mechanism that they require. The style should also be chosen with the design and decoration of the room in mind. The selection below gives an idea of the variety of styles.

Porcelain knob

Brass knob

Chrome knob

Brass pull handle

Wrought-iron pull handle

Wrought-iron lever
handle with lock

Porcelain
finger plate

Nylon
keyhole plate

Brass-covered
keyhole plate

Designer lever
handle with lock

Brass lever handle
with lock

Stainless-steel
lever handle

Chrome lever handle
on concealed rose

CHANGING DOOR HARDWARE

Most handles are held in place by retaining screws that go directly into the face of the door. However, in some cases, small setscrews are used to secure the handle in position. Whatever the design, it is usually easy to determine how the handle is fixed in place and how to remove it.

1 Remove the old lever handle with a screwdriver. If you are going to replace the corresponding handle on the other side of the door, remove that one as well.

2 Fill the old screw holes with all-purpose filler, and sand it to a smooth finish when it is dry. Leave the old spindle in place as this is already cut to the right size for the door; only replace it if the new door hardware will not fit it.

3 Position the new door knob on the door and make pilot holes for the new screws with a bradawl. Remove the new knob.

4 Paint over the repaired screw holes and leave to dry. Secure the new knob in position, inserting the screws into the pilot holes.

WINDOW FURNITURE

A s with door furniture (or hardware), there is a wide choice of styles and types of fixtures for use on windows. Window mechanisms tend to vary a bit more than those for doors, so it is important to choose fixtures that will operate correctly on your particular window.

CHOOSING A STYLE OF WINDOW HARDWARE

Always remember the practical issues when choosing a style of window hardware—just because something looks good, doesn't necessarily mean it will be easy to use. Try and choose something that will complement the color and design of other accessories in the room—the door hardware especially—as this will help to create a balanced decorative scheme.

Fanlight catch

Wrought-iron fanlight opener

Fanlight catch plate

Brass screw-up casement stay

Wrought-iron stay and pins

Brass casement fastener

Brass opening stay and fastener

Telescopic friction casement stay

Locking steel casement fastener

Wrought-iron casement fastener

Locking chrome casement fastener

Brass sash fastener with ceramic knob

Brass sash lift

Brass stay and pins

CHANGING CASEMENT WINDOW HARDWARE

As long as you make sure the window hardware you buy is suited to the design of the windows in your home, the attachment process is relatively straightforward. Casement windows are usually secured with fasteners along the side and with stays and pins along the bottom of the casement frame.

1 Remove the old fasteners. Hold the new ones in place and mark the position for the new screw holes with a pencil. Draw a line around the fastener catch to see if it will need to be recessed slightly into the frame.

2 If it is necessary to cut a recess for the fastener catch, use a chisel to cut out the recess in the window frame. Be careful to remove shavings of wood only as far as the pencil guideline—do not go beyond it.

3 Make pilot holes for the fastener catch plate with a bradawl. Screw it in tightly in position in the recess.

4 Make two more pilot holes for the fastener itself, then screw that in place on the window.

STAYS AND PINS

For the stays and pins, use a similar procedure to that used for fasteners (see the steps above). However, it is not necessary to recess the pins into the window frame. Fill all the old fixing holes made for the previous window hardware and paint the repaired area before attaching the new fixtures.

SECURITY FIXTURES

S ecurity should always be considered when making improvements. Windows and doors are two areas where these considerations are particularly appropriate, since it is always possible to update or add to the security systems you are using. Although security is the main concern when installing these devices, it is possible to use systems that do not detract too much from the room decoration.

WINDOW SECURITY

Most home security is based on a system of deterrents—although window locks may not deter the most determined of intruders, they certainly ward off the casual ones. Installing window locks is a simple process that can be carried out very quickly.

| Remove the old pins from the window frame and then replace them with locking pins that match the finish to your existing stays.

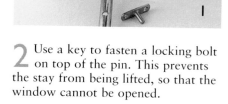

2 Use a key to fasten a locking bolt on top of the pin. This prevents the stay from being lifted, so that the window cannot be opened.

Casement locks: screw one part of the lock into the casement frame and the other into the window frame. A key is used to clamp the two parts of the lock together, preventing the window from being opened. This lock can be installed in minutes with four screws. For extra security on large windows, have one lock at the top part of the casement and one at the bottom.

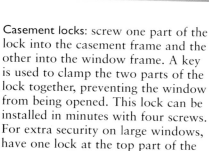

DOOR SECURITY

Exterior doors should always have a key locking system, whether it be a mortise deadbolt lock, cylinder lock, or other similar security feature. Always change the locks when you move into a new house, since you can never be sure how many people have had access to the existing set of keys. In addition to secure locks, there are other simple security measures that can be used to back up the primary locking systems on the door. These help to provide peace of mind by adding to the overall security of your home. Some of the simplest measures to install are peepholes or viewers, door chains, and mortise door bolts. Peepholes or viewers are the best way of seeing who is knocking at the door without having to open it. They come in a range of sizes, so choose an appropriate one for your door. Door chains allow you to see who is outside while opening the door only a little.

1 Drill a hole in the door the same size as the threaded part of the peephole. Insert half of the peephole on the exterior side of the door.

2 From the inside of the door, join it up with the other half of the peephole. Use the flat edge of a screwdriver to tighten it.

Mortise door bolts: these should be positioned at the top and bottom of the door. They take a little longer to fit than standard door bolts, but they tend to provide better security. The locking system is operated with a special key.

Door chains: these chains can be fitted quickly with just a few screws, and they offer extra protection when opening the door to strangers.

CURTAIN TRACKS

Tracks are one of the simplest mechanisms for hanging curtains or draperies. They are designed purely as functional items and have no real aesthetic value since the curtain heading covers the track once it has been installed. Although track design varies, most work on the principle of using a number of specially designed plastic brackets that hold the track securely in place.

ATTACHING THE TRACK BRACKETS

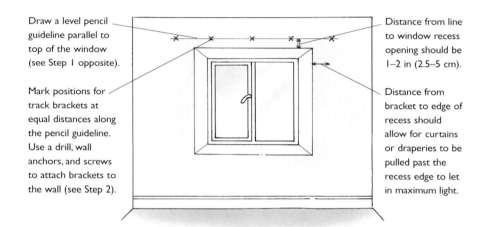

Draw a level pencil guideline parallel to top of the window (see Step 1 opposite).

Mark positions for track brackets at equal distances along the pencil guideline. Use a drill, wall anchors, and screws to attach brackets to the wall (see Step 2).

Distance from line to window recess opening should be 1–2 in (2.5–5 cm).

Distance from bracket to edge of recess should allow for curtains or draperies to be pulled past the recess edge to let in maximum light.

ATTACHING THE TRACK

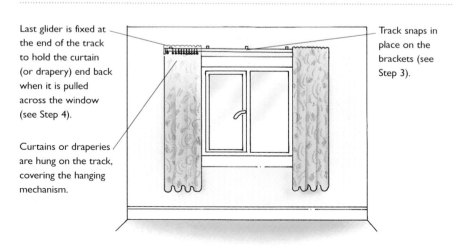

Last glider is fixed at the end of the track to hold the curtain (or drapery) end back when it is pulled across the window (see Step 4).

Curtains or draperies are hung on the track, covering the hanging mechanism.

Track snaps in place on the brackets (see Step 3).

INSTALLING A TRACK

Tracks can be attached directly to the window frame, but this will cut down the distance the curtains or draperies may be drawn back from the window, especially when the window is recessed as shown here. Attachment on the wall surface, outside the recess, is usually the best option.

1 Use a level to draw a line above the window recess, parallel to the top of the recess and the ceiling. Bracket positions may then be marked out along this line to ensure that the track will run straight, without any kinks or bends.

2 Secure the track brackets to the wall, making sure that they are the right way up. The brackets must be attached securely in place so that they are able to take the weight of both the track and the curtains or draperies.

3 Clip the track onto the brackets, then tighten up the retaining screws on the brackets to make sure that the track cannot fall off and that it is secure enough to take the weight of the curtains.

4 Hang the required number of gliders on each end of the track, before securing the final gliders in place at each end of the track. Touch in any visible pencil marks on the wall with the appropriate paint and leave to dry. The curtains can now be hung on the gliders.

CURTAIN POLES

C urtain poles are a more decorative alternative to curtain tracks. The curtains are hung from rings rather than gliders, with the idea that the poles are meant to be seen and form part of the window dressing decoration. Poles are usually wooden but some are made from metal or plastic composites.

ATTACHING THE POLE BRACKETS

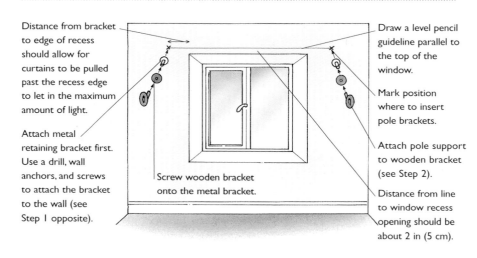

Distance from bracket to edge of recess should allow for curtains to be pulled past the recess edge to let in the maximum amount of light.

Attach metal retaining bracket first. Use a drill, wall anchors, and screws to attach the bracket to the wall (see Step 1 opposite).

Draw a level pencil guideline parallel to the top of the window.

Mark position where to insert pole brackets.

Attach pole support to wooden bracket (see Step 2).

Distance from line to window recess opening should be about 2 in (5 cm).

Screw wooden bracket onto the metal bracket.

ATTACHING THE POLE

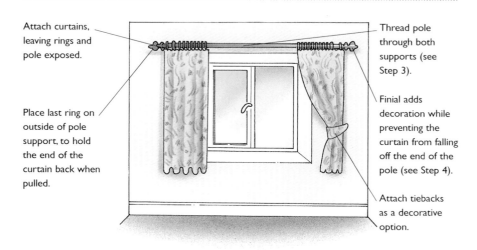

Attach curtains, leaving rings and pole exposed.

Place last ring on outside of pole support, to hold the end of the curtain back when pulled.

Thread pole through both supports (see Step 3).

Finial adds decoration while preventing the curtain from falling off the end of the pole (see Step 4).

Attach tiebacks as a decorative option.

INSTALLING A CURTAIN POLE

Curtain poles are simple to install since they usually have just two wall fixings (though longer poles may require more). However, the brackets and pole must be positioned correctly; if they are not level, the curtains will hang unevenly, spoiling the finished look.

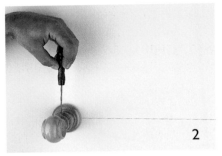

1 Once a level guideline has been drawn (see page 19, Step 1), attach the metal retaining brackets at the end of the guideline. Make sure that the threaded central column of the bracket is positioned precisely on the pencil guideline.

2 Screw the wooden bracket onto the metal one and fit the pole support into the wooden bracket. Fix the pole support in position by tightening the retaining screw on top of the wooden bracket, screwing it through into the pole support.

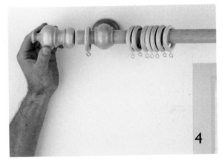

3 Thread the curtain pole into the wooden pole supports.

4 Once rings have been threaded onto the pole, attach a finial to each end. These prevent the final rings from falling off the end of the pole and add a decorative touch.

DOUBLE GLAZING

Double glazing on windows reduces heat loss, sound transmission, and the buildup of condensation, thereby acting as an efficiency mechanism for the whole household. It uses two panes of glass, separated by an air gap, in place of the standard single pane. The opening and closing mechanism on double-glazed units is more efficient than that of single-glazed units. Double-glazed windows differ in style, quality, and efficiency, so it is important to weigh these differences when deciding on the best system for your needs.

CHOOSING A STYLE OF DOUBLE-GLAZED WINDOW

The early days of double glazing provided unimaginative functional units, aimed at efficiency rather than any aesthetic appeal. In recent years, this position has changed and double-glazed-window manufacturers now provide a wide range of styles to suit all tastes. The major criticism of double glazing has sometimes been its lack of character, but nowadays it is possible to install units that give the appearance of more traditional, and arguably more attractive, designs. Natural wood double-glazed windows, for instance, are becoming increasingly popular. These are usually made from hardwood.

PVC frames: these window units are low maintenance while providing excellent heat-retaining qualities and reduced sound transmission from outside. They are easily cleaned and require no painting, inside or out. They are also very secure, with most designs having locking casements.

Dealing with doors: units that replace existing door systems, whether they be front or back doors, or sliding patio units as shown in this example, may have an aluminum finish that requires very little maintenance, but provides maximum efficiency.

DOUBLE GLAZING CHOICES

- Entire windows: double-glazed units in a PVC frame are a common option for people renovating their home. This tends to be the most expensive option because all the windows in the house are usually replaced at the same time because replacing single windows has little effect on efficiency. Although expensive in the short term, savings will be made in the long term. It does require more advanced do-it-yourself skills to install these.
- Real wood double-glazed windows: these cross the barrier between traditional windows and earlier, less attractive versions. Hardwood double-glazed windows require only coats of stain or varnish from time to time as maintenance.
- Single-sealed units: as an option to replacing entire windows, frames and all, it is possible just to replace the glass itself with single double-glazed units. The existing frames do need a large rebated area to fit these thick

panes, but as long as they are of sufficient size, the process is a simple matter of replacing the old single panes with the new double units.
- Secondary double glazing: this involves attaching glazed units to the existing windows. The old frame is used as the base on which large panes of glass, secured in a PVC frame, are attached. They are usually hinged to allow you access to the original window. These units are less of a job than total replacement with double-glazed window units.
- The budget option: the simplest form of double glazing is to use proprietary plastic film or sheeting, secured around the window frame with double-sided tape. Going over the positioned film or sheeting with a hair dryer tightens it slightly to give a taut, neat final appearance. The drawback is that it is not possible to get to the windows to open them, so this method should only be used if this limitation is acceptable.

INSULATING

I nsulation plays an important role in retaining heat in a house, as well as eliminating drafts and creating a more efficient home. Double-glazed windows play an important part in this process, but it is also possible to target other areas that benefit from insulation. The cost of insulation can range from a few dollars to a very large sum of money, depending on the scale of the work and the available budget.

AREAS TO INSULATE

Attics

Attics are one of the most important areas to insulate because a great deal of heat can be lost through the roof of your home. You can use loose-fill insulation, which takes the form of granules that are poured between the joists in the roof space, or blanket insulation. Blanket insulation (shown opposite) tends to be a neater process with large areas being covered quickly and at relatively low cost.

Floor

The space between floor levels can also be insulated. This involves taking up the floorboards, so it can be a fairly lengthy project. However, it can be beneficial, especially if the floor in question is above a basement.

Walls

In new houses, the exterior walls are insulated; in older houses, this may not be the case. External cavity walls are insulated by an injection process; an insulating chemical is forced, under pressure, through a number of drilled holes into the cavity. Once completed, the holes are filled. This technique is really the domain of the professionals,

and is one area where you should seek a specialist's advice and help. When erecting new internal stud walls, blanket insulation can be used inside the cavity during construction.

Doors

Doors can be fitted with antidraft strips to make them more efficient barriers once they are closed. This form of insulation is relatively simple to install and can be carried out very quickly (see opposite).

Windows

Aside from double glazing, a window's insulating efficiency can be improved by using antidraft strips in a similar manner to that used for doors, to reduce the flow of air around the edges of the windows. Curtains are good window insulation, especially if they are thick ones or have an insulating lining.

Pipes

All pipes in the attic must be insulated to protect them from the effects of extreme cold temperatures. Insulation specially designed for this purpose is easy to install and relatively inexpensive (see opposite).

USING INSULATING MATERIALS

Insulating materials are by design fairly unattractive. In most cases this is not a problem for the overall look of your home because the insulation is hidden from view. However, in places where it can be seen—such as around windows or doors—try to make sure that the insulation is installed as neatly as possible. With the less structured methods of insulation, the installation process is fairly simple. It can be achieved in a relatively short space of time and the beneficial effect will be very noticeable, but it is necessary to stick to a few straightforward rules in order to gain the maximum benefit from your efforts.

Blanket insulation: this insulation is manufactured in rolls and is applied between the joists in the attic. Because it can irritate the skin, you need to wear a dust mask, protective gloves, and a long-sleeved shirt when rolling it out. Be careful not to crush the blanket since much of its effectiveness is in its depth. Position it very lightly, rather than forcing it.

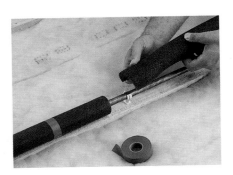

Pipe insulation tubes: those pipes in the attic that are not covered by blanket insulation (see above) must be covered with pipe insulation. Always use the pipe insulation tubes specially designed for this process. They open along one side, allowing you to mold a tube around the entire pipe. Secure the pipe tubes in place with tape—this is especially important at joints and corners.

Draft eliminators: draft eliminators for doors consist of a metal or plastic fixing plate with a fibrous brush strip. The strip can be attached to the door with screws. Make sure that the ends of the bristles overlap onto the floor surface when the door is closed, thus preventing a draft. Because the bristles on the brush strip are flexible, they allow the door to be opened easily but retain the draft-eliminating properties when shut.

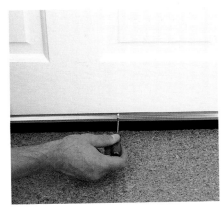

ALARMS

H ousehold alarm systems were often considered to be an optional choice, but in recent times their popularity has escalated. The growth of this market has resulted in a range of systems that can be easily installed, rather than having to turn to professional installers.

BURGLAR ALARMS

All burglar alarms are based on a system of sensors that either detect room movement or are alerted when contacts are broken around house entrances. Once a contact is broken or sensor alerted, a siren raises the alarm. A wired system requires the components or sensors in the system to be connected and relayed back to the control panel. A non-wired system doesn't need a physical connection between the sensors and the control panel, although there may need to be a connection from the control panel to the outside siren.

SMOKE ALARMS

These are essential in every household. They should be positioned at ceiling level outside bedrooms, to wake occupants in an emergency, and any areas where a fire might start. Smoke alarms wired into the electricity supply should be left to an electrician. However, battery-operated ones are simple to install.

1 Unhinge the lid of the battery-operated alarm and mark the position of the two screw holes on the ceiling with a pencil. Drill two pilot holes and position wall anchors, if necessary. Hold the alarm back in position and secure it with screws inserted in each drilled hole.

2 Once the alarm is in position, insert the battery, close the lid, and test the alarm following the manufacturer's guidelines.

CARBON MONOXIDE ALARMS

This form of alarm is becoming more popular due to a greater awareness of the risks of carbon monoxide poisoning. They are simple to install—most designs simply need to be plugged into the electricity supply.

Adding Character

ADDING CHARACTER

Once refurbishment of the essential fixtures is complete, it is time to turn to the areas of your home where you can be more creative in your attempts to add character and style. While most houses have the essential basics, improving on them can produce a much more comfortable living environment, which reflects your personal preferences and tastes. Many changes can be achieved with very straightforward projects that can be completed in a relatively short time. This chapter highlights possible areas for improvement and demonstrates how simple changes can be very effective, illustrating that it is not always necessary to undertake major structural work in order to achieve an exciting new look.

WOODEN RAILS

A dding a picture rail or dado trim to a room is one way of breaking up wall surfaces and adding interest to the decoration as a whole. A picture rail is particularly appropriate in rooms with high ceilings since it can be used to help bring down the level of the ceiling. Wooden dado trim can be used in nearly all rooms and makes an excellent division for separating different wall finishes and colors, or it can be seen simply as a design feature in its own right.

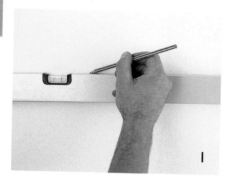

1 Draw a level guideline around the perimeter of the room. For dado trim, a suitable position is one yard (meter) from the floor.

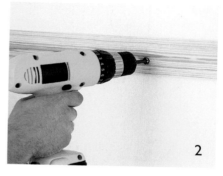

2 Hold the dado trim with its base along the pencil guideline and drill through it into the wall. Open up the entrance to the drilled hole with a countersink drill bit.

3 Insert a wall anchor and screw, knocking it into place with a hammer. Leave about one-third of the length of the screw visible.

4 Screw it into place, ensuring that the head of the screw sits below the level of the wood.

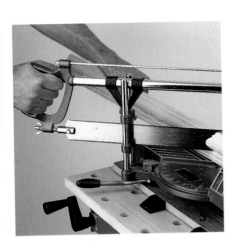

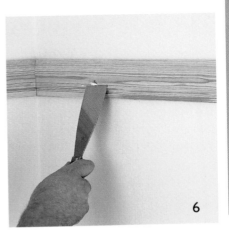

2

5 Measure and cut any corners in the trim using a miter saw.

6 Fill the screwhead holes using all-purpose filler. Apply it so that it is slightly higher than the surface to allow for shrinkage as it dries.

7 Sand the filled holes to give them a smooth finish that is level with the rest of the wooden trim.

8 Run a bead of caulking around the top and bottom edges of the trim and along the corner junctions, then smooth it with a wet finger to give a neat finish, ready for painting.

BASEBOARDS

Most rooms need baseboards because they act as the decorative trim or division between walls and floors. There are different styles of baseboard—your choice is a matter of personal preference. It is a straightforward job to remove existing baseboards and replace them with new, and although it might be necessary to redecorate wall surfaces afterward, this can be seen as part of the remodeling process.

CUTTING CORNERS

In order to fit new baseboards, you need to be able to cut corners in it. Internal corners are cut in exactly the same way as dado trim (see page 29). At external corners, the baseboards should be measured and attached as shown below.

1 To measure the corner accurately, position the baseboard for one wall at a time in place, and mark the exact apex of the corner on the board with a pencil.

2 Using a miter block or specially designed miter saw, cut the marked lengths of baseboard.

3 Hold the two mitered joints together at the external corner by nailing brads along the joint. This will prevent the baseboard joint from easing open over time.

SCRIBING BASEBOARDS

Floors that undulate, or are not level, can pose a problem because the factory-made edge of the baseboard will not sit flush along the floor surface. This makes it necessary to fit the bottom edge of the baseboard more precisely to the uneven floor profile. This is achieved by a process known as "scribing."

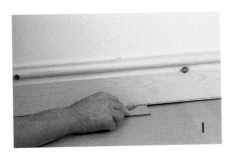

2

1 Cut a small block of wood the same height as the largest gap between the base of the baseboard and the floor. Hold a pencil on top of the block and run the block along the entire length, making a guideline that should imitate the curvature of the floor.

2 Clamp the baseboard to the workbench, and use a wood plane to remove shavings of wood as far as the pencil guideline. Attach the baseboard to the wall, with the base of the length of board flush with the undulating profile of the floor.

SECURING BASEBOARDS

Baseboards can be secured with nails or screws, depending on the nature of the wall that it is being fixed to. Wire nails are ideal for drywall, whereas masonry nails are ideal for solid block walls, although there can be a tendency for baseboards to "bounce" away from the wall surface if the nails do not hold it securely. Wall anchors and screws, although more time consuming, tend to produce a firmer, longer-lasting attachment.

Using screws: drill some pilot holes and use all-purpose concrete anchor screws, or wall anchors and screws as shown here. Knock the anchor and screw into place with a hammer before finally screwing tightly in position.

Using nails: make sure that you punch in nails after they have been hammered in. This way the holes can be filled and sanded to a flat, smooth surface before the baseboards are painted.

PANELING

P aneling is another method of adding character to wall surfaces. It can be applied over entire walls, or just up to dado level. Most paneling needs to be secured to a framework that acts as a level base, otherwise any slight unevenness in a wall surface will be accentuated by the finished panel.

2 MAKING A FRAME

A framework needs to be substantial enough to support the paneling, but not so intrusive that it brings the paneling too far away from the wall surface. The ideal material for frame construction is 2-by-1-in (5-by-2.5-cm) battens.

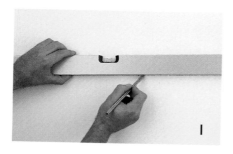

1

2

1 Make a level pencil guideline on the wall at the height you want your paneling to reach.

2 Attach a length of wooden batten horizontally, using the pencil line as a guide for the top of the batten.

3 Continue to add battens down the wall, ensuring that they all run parallel. For dado paneling, three or four battens are all that are required. Make sure that the bottom batten sits close to the floor surface.

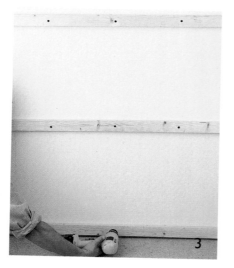

3

INSTALLING PANELING

There are different types of paneling available, but tongue-and-groove provides an effective and neat finish. It can either be applied as single strips, joined to make a continuous surface, or specially routed medium-density-fiberboard (MDF) sheets can be cut down to size and installed.

Secret nailing: apply single tongue-and-groove lengths vertically, slotting the groove of each new length over the tongue of the previous one. Secure each length in position by nailing at a 45-degree angle through the tongue and into the wooden batten below. Use a punch to push the nailhead below the surface of the wood, so that every fixing is hidden when the next tongue-and-groove length along is added.

2

Using sheets: large sheets of tongue-and-groove MDF paneling can be used to cover frameworks very quickly, but they can be more expensive, so you need to weigh the cost against the time advantage.

FINISHING OFF

Whichever type of paneling is used, you will always need to make finishing touches to complete the finished effect before you decorate it. As well as adding baseboard to the base of the paneling, creating a decorative edge at dado trim height is also important.

1 Attach another length of batten along the top edge of the paneling. Screw it directly into the top horizontal batten used for the initial frame.

2 Pin a half-round decorative molding to the front edge of the batten to create an attractive curved edge. Fill the paneling surface and edges, as required, before decorating.

COVES

In much the same way that baseboards add a decorative edge at floor level, coves complement this finish at ceiling level. They also round off the sharp edge of a wall/ceiling junction, giving a more elegant and shapely look to a wall surface. There are many different types and styles of cove available—they can be made from Styrofoam, or various plaster bases, but the most authentic period styles tend to be made from fibrous plaster. Always use the adhesive recommended by the manufacturer for applying coves to the ceiling. The tricky part of cove application is mitering the corners, whether external or internal. However, manufacturers usually supply a custom-made template or miter block, which can be used for making whichever miter is required for a particular joint.

1 Measure the length of cove required and cut it to size, using the miter block positioned across the cove width. Keep the saw tight against the block as you cut, to ensure the correct angle of cut and gradient through the length of cove.

2 Apply cove adhesive generously to the top and bottom edges of the length. A scraper is the ideal tool for applying the adhesive.

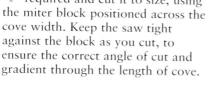

3 Press the length of cove firmly in position at the wall/ceiling junction, making sure that the edge of the cove on the ceiling extends onto the ceiling the same distance as the edge of the cove on the wall extends onto the wall.

2

4 Hammer in a number of nails below the cove to support its weight while it dries.

5 Use a damp sponge to remove excess adhesive from the cove surface before it dries.

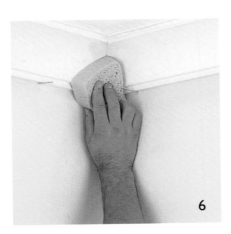

6 Fill in all the cracks at the ceiling and wall junction with adhesive. Fill any gaps at the mitered junction of the corner once the next length of cove has been applied.

7 Once the adhesive is dry, remove the supporting nails and fill any holes. Finally, sand away any rough areas of adhesive before decorating the walls and ceiling.

PLASTER FRAMES AND ROSES

O ther plaster-based accessories that can be used to add character to rooms include frames and ceiling roses. Most are applied with cove adhesive, but some need extra support to keep them in place.

2 MAKING A FRAME

Plaster frames are a good way of highlighting features, or creating display areas on a wall space. They can be used around alcoves to add greater depth; on a flat wall area, they can be painted to provide an excellent decorative detail on an otherwise bland surface.

1 Draw a wall panel with a pencil, ensuring that it is totally square by using a level.

2 Cut the horizontal and vertical lengths to size, apply adhesive, and position them using the pencil lines as guides. Hammer in nails to support each length, as required.

3 Apply adhesive to the corner blocks and position them. Once the frame has dried, remove the nails and fill any holes, as required.

ATTACHING A CEILING ROSE

Options for ceiling decoration are often limited, but adding a plaster rose is
one way of adding extra interest to the vast open area that is characteristic of
most ceilings. Lightweight plaster roses can be secured using cove adhesive,
but heavy-duty ones need the extra support of screws as well, to hold them in
position on the ceiling. The screws must be screwed into ceiling joists.

2

1 Use a joist detector to find the
position and direction of the
ceiling joists. Using this information,
mark the ideal position for your
ceiling rose—usually this is in the
center of the room.

2 Apply generous amounts of the
cove adhesive to the back of the
ceiling rose, being careful to cover
it completely.

3 Position the rose on the ceiling
and drill through it into the
ceiling joist, using a screw for fixing.
Repeat this process all around the
circumference of the rose, fixing a
screw in any area that the detector
shows to have joist support.

4 Fill all the screw holes with some
all-purpose filler, to create a neat
finish on the ceiling rose, then sand
with fine-grade sandpaper for a
smooth finish.

DOORS

D oors help to form the overall look of a room, and they should be considered as one of the main features in the room. As well as performing their functional role, they can make a style statement. In this way, they can contribute dramatically to the decorative scheme.

CHOOSING A DOOR STYLE

Door decoration, such as leaded windowpanes, or the way they are painted is often the most influential factor in their appearance. Doors that have a large wooden surface area lend themselves to various paint or natural wood finishes that show them off to good effect.

The rustic look: old doors often need little decoration— their natural grain plus the effects of wear and tear over a long period of time produce a very authentic, rustic appearance.

Using glass: doors that contain glass panels or panes let more light into rooms, whether the doors are exterior or interior ones. Using leaded windowpanes or colored glass can also create an attractive and individual look.

Paint effects: any number of door finishes can be created with paint effects—a marbled finish is a very inventive way of producing a new and interesting look.

STICKING DOORS

Whatever doors you choose to have in your home, it is essential that they open and close smoothly. In modern houses, because central heating is common and makes temperatures vary, doors can expand and contract over time. Slight structural movement of the house can also lead to doors sticking and becoming difficult to open. Fortunately, this is a simple problem to solve.

1 Make a pencil guideline along the edge of the door in the places where it is sticking. This can be done by holding the shaft of the pencil against your finger as you run it down the edge of the door to produce a straight line.

2 Use a wood plane to shave away the edge of the door as far as the pencil guideline. If the door is sticking closer to the bottom, it may be necessary to take it off its hinges to plane it.

LOOSE DOORS

The opposite problem may occur where a door fails to shut properly because it has shrunk slightly. Since it is not easy to add wood to the edge of the door, an alternative method is required. The hinges can be built out from the doorstop, or, as shown here, the striking plate can be built out slightly in order to engage the latch and close the door.

1 Unscrew the striking plate from the door frame. Cut a piece of thick, stiff cardboard the same size as the striking plate and position it on the door frame before reattaching the plate.

2 When the plate is screwed back in place, use a craft knife to cut out the central area of cardboard to allow the latch to close. You may find that you need to experiment and add more cardboard until the door shuts firmly.

2

RENOVATING FLUSH DOORS

F lush doors have very little character and they benefit from some form of refurbishment to add an extra dimension to their bland appearance. Repainting the door or changing the handles are two simple methods of remodeling the look of a flush door. For a more dramatic transformation, you can add panels to its surface.

ADDING PANELS

When adding panels to a door, you need to work out how many panels you want on it, and whether the panel sizes will vary across the door surface.

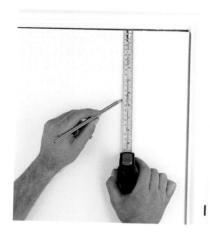

1

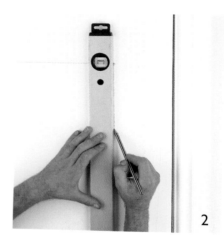

2

1 Mark out the panel sizes on the door, penciling in the corner positions of each panel. Take time to double check the measurements as any mistakes will be very obvious on the finished door.

3

2 Using a level, join up all the corner measurements and provide a complete pencil guideline for the panel layout. For a crooked door frame or a sloping room, you may need to adjust the level of the panels by eye and balance their position against the unlevel elements of the door position.

3 Use a miter saw to cut molding beads down to the required size. Use some fine-grade abrasive paper to sand the cut edge to remove any rough areas before attaching them.

4 Attach double-sided tape to the back of each molding in turn, applying the tape along the central area of the molding.

5 Stick the molding in position along the pencil guideline on the door. There will be a little time to adjust its position before the tape adheres to the door permanently. Once positioned correctly, press firmly on the molding to ensure a strong bond.

6 Continue to add moldings until all the panels are complete. Finally seal along the edge of each molding with decorator's caulking, using a wet finger to smooth it to a neat finish. Paint the door once the caulking is dry.

PANEL TRANSFORMATION
Panels can totally change the look of a flush door. The moldings can be painted the same color as the main body of the door, as shown here, or they can be picked out in a contrasting color for an impressive effect.

FIREPLACES

Fireplaces—whether they are used or not—create an attractive focal point in a room and revamping your old fireplace or installing a new one is a good way of changing the look of a room. Installing an inactive fireplace and mantel is a simple job that requires little time and endeavor. Some fireplaces are supplied by manufacturers in kit form; alternatively, you can build one from your own plan.

2

LAYING A HEARTH

Most fireplaces require a hearth area in order to complete the effect. This can simply be a cutaway section out of the carpet, or a material such as a marble slab can be laid to make a hearth, but this will need to be secured in place with mortar, as shown below.

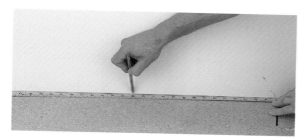

1 Measure along the wall to find the central point for the position of the marble slab. A fireplace tends to look best when it is centered on the wall.

2 Mix some mortar (five parts sand to one part cement). Add water to make it a firm but smooth consistency. Place six fist-size piles of mortar, one at each corner and the two midpoints of where the slab is to be positioned.

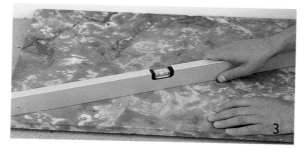

3 Position the marble slab, twisting the slab slightly as you bed it into the mortar. Use a level to make sure that the slab is sitting perfectly level across all dimensions.

ATTACHING THE FACING

If you are not using a kit-form mantel, it is possible to buy complete fire facings that are quite simple to attach to the wall. When choosing a mantel, make sure that its base dimensions match the width dimension of the hearth area, so that a neat, balanced effect is achieved.

Screwing in position: a wooden mantel can be secured with two to four screw fixings. Depending on the design, try and hide the fixing points so that they are not obvious when the mantel is in place. The best method is to attach a glass plate fixing to the back of the mantel and then fix through this into the wall.

2

REAL FIRE FACINGS

Installing a mantel for a real fire, or installing a real fireplace on its own, is a longer process. The extent of work that is required will depend on your choice of fuel.

- Gas fireplaces: these have a real fire effect without the need to clear away ashes, or physically lay and light the fire. A gas supply is essential, as is a flue or an existing chimney. Once installed, a gas fire is an efficient, attractive asset to a room, but there does need to be some planning before installation. All such fireplaces should be supplied with regulations and manufacturer's instructions.
- Electric fireplaces: like the gas fireplaces, these are made to imitate the effect of a real fire, but use electricity as their power source. No flue or combustible fuel supply is needed.
- Solid fuel: changing the hearth or the mantel around an existing solid-fuel fireplace can be simple or complex, depending on the fireplace design. Seek professional advice before working on complex designs.

THE DRESSED LOOK
Once fixed in place, a simple combination of a hearth and mantel makes an excellent focal point in any room.

TEXTURED PLASTER

A dding texture to wall surfaces is an easy way of adding character to a room. This can be achieved by paint effects or embossed wallpapers, but by far the most authentic way is to actually add a coat of textured plaster to the walls. Proprietary brands of textured plaster are available or you can achieve the finish with simple one-coat plaster. The wall can be painted, or color-washed, to add depth to the surface.

2

APPLYING TEXTURED PLASTER

One-coat plaster can be applied over rough or smooth surfaces with equal effect. Make sure that the floor is covered with drop cloths since some plaster will fall away as it squeezes out around the edge of the plaster float.

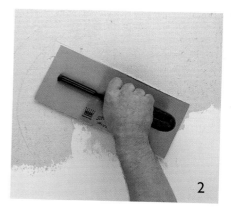

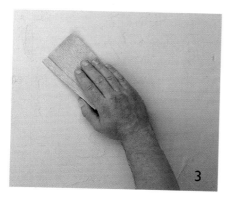

1 Apply a general-purpose builder's sealant to the surface of the wall to prime and seal it.

2 Mix some plaster to a firm, pastelike consistency. Apply it to the wall with a plaster float, using large sweeping motions. Combine moving the float across the surface with firm downward pressure. Leave grooves and ruts in the surface of the plaster to ensure a textured finish.

3 Once the plaster has dried, use fine-grade abrasive paper to remove any high points on the finish—these will only fall away with time so it is best to remove them before decorating. The surface can then be painted, or you can use a paint effect such as a color-wash.

Renovating Floors

RENOVATING FLOORS

Floors are an important consideration when remodeling your home because they cover a large surface area and therefore have a major influence on the look of rooms and their overall decorative effect. Refurbishment can be a simple matter of replacing the carpet or vinyl. For a more dramatic effect, you can change the look completely. When choosing a floorcovering, remember to consider the rest of the decoration in the room, as well as the practical aspects of the flooring you select. This chapter contains many options for floor renovation, both minor and more adventurous, and it explains the best techniques for preparing a floor surface for a revamp plus various finishing techniques.

3

SANDING FLOORS

To create any sort of finish on bare floorboards you generally need to sand them first to provide a good surface for the decoration. For a large area, it is worth renting a drum floor sander. Before using the sander, make sure that the floor is totally clear of obstacles and that any protruding nails are punched in below the surface.

ORDER OF WORK

In order to produce an even finish, it is important to stick to a particular sequence of work when using a drum sander.

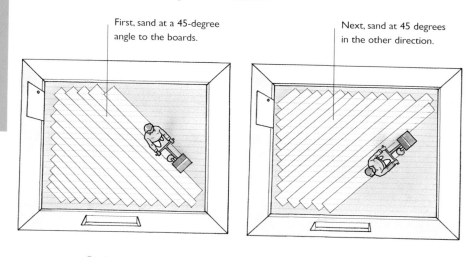

First, sand at a 45-degree angle to the boards.

Next, sand at 45 degrees in the other direction.

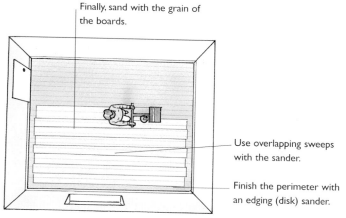

Finally, sand with the grain of the boards.

Use overlapping sweeps with the sander.

Finish the perimeter with an edging (disk) sander.

3

USING A FLOOR SANDER

Floor sanders are fairly straightforward to use as long as you follow the manufacturer's instructions and the directions shown opposite. Make sure that you wear a dust mask because the machine causes a lot of mess.

Starting the sander: tip the sander back slightly before starting it, otherwise the sanding drum will dig into the floor surface. Once started, lower it gently onto the floor and work with an even pace in the required direction. Do not linger in one area for any length of time.

Grades of sandpaper: depending on the nature of the floor, you may need to use different grades of sandpaper. To remove several layers of old coatings, begin with a coarse grade of sandpaper and gradually work down to a fine grade.

3

USING AN EDGING SANDER

Edging (disk) sanders are used to get close to the baseboard and reach the areas that cannot be covered by the larger drum sander. They are also messy, so it is still essential to wear a dust mask.

Sanding technique: hold on tightly to the handles of the sander, since they can produce quite a kick as they progress across the floor surface. Allow the edge of the sanding pad to get right up to the floor edge in order to remove the old coatings.

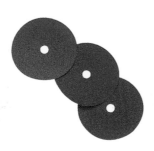

Grades of sandpaper: an edging sander works with an orbital action and uses round sheets of sandpaper. Again, gradually reduce the grade of sandpaper as you remove all the old layers of paint and/or varnish from the floor.

STAINING AND VARNISHING

S tain and varnish give a hardwearing coating while allowing the natural grain of the wood to show through. Traditionally, stains and varnishes were fairly limited in their choice of color and finish, but in recent years the range has increased to include all sorts of options for the final look of a stained or varnished floor.

TECHNIQUE

Varnish can be applied to floorboards as a finish in its own right, following the steps below. Stains usually need to be protected with coats of varnish after they have been applied. Always read the manufacturer's guidelines to check that the stain or varnish you have bought is suitable for floor use—some may not have the hardwearing properties that are essential for floor coatings.

1 Clean the entire floor surface with a cotton rag dampened with mineral spirits. This removes dust and debris and, once the mineral spirit evaporates, it leaves a totally clean and particle-free surface.

2 Apply stain with the grain of the wood, brushing it out thoroughly to ensure even coverage. Treat each floorboard as a separate surface, otherwise the overlaps in stain from one board to another will show up as rather patchy and ruin the finish. Apply extra coats of stain, if they are needed—two full coats is usually sufficient for floorboards.

3 Once the stain is totally dry, apply varnish to seal and protect the stain finish. Again, brush with the grain of the wood, ensuring that the varnish covers the entire floor surface. A second, and sometimes third, coat will be required to give the floor surface a tough and hardwearing finish. When applying coats of varnish, sand the wood lightly between each coat.

VARYING COLOR AND PATTERN

When staining floorboards, it is possible to be quite adventurous and achieve a more extravagant look, or simply a very individual one. Color can be used to add greater vibrancy to a floor finish, and this idea can be taken one step further if some sort of pattern is also introduced into the design.

1 Stain every other row of boards with the same color—a vivid blue makes a change from more traditional natural wood colors.

2 Once the blue has dried, apply a strong contrasting color to the other boards in order to produce a simple striped effect. Apply extra coats, if necessary, as well as varnish to protect the finished floor.

ALTERNATIVE NATURAL WOOD FLOOR FINISHES

There are various alternatives to stain and varnish for producing a natural wood floor finish.

- Wax: this is one of the more traditional finishes for floors. Wax produces an excellent effect, especially on older floorboards, which tend to have more character than modern equivalents. However, waxing floors can be an arduous process requiring frequent recoating and buffing for the floor to look really good. Using a proprietary sealer on the bare wood surface before waxing reduces the number of wax coats required to produce a good finish.

- Stain varnishes: there are proprietary stain varnishes that can be used as an all-in-one floor treatment. These are applied to the floorboards in the usual way, but require no varnish coatings as final protection.

- Water-based alternatives: traditional floor coatings have always been oil-based. They take a long time to dry between coats and make the overall process fairly lengthy. Nowadays, when choosing floor finishes, there are various water-based products to choose from. These are just as durable but their shorter drying time means that the job can be completed much more quickly.

LAYING A SUBFLOOR

S ubfloors, as their name suggests, are a base on which finishing floorcoverings are laid, although they can be painted to provide a finished look in their own right (see page 53). They are most often used to smooth over a previous floorcovering in readiness for the new one. Hardboard, particleboard, and plywood can all be used for a subfloor.

LAYING HARDBOARD

Hardboard is a thin, flexible board that is used to cover floorboards and provide a sound surface for a new floorcovering. It is supplied in large and small sheets—the smaller 4-by-2-foot (120-by-60-cm) sheets are easiest to use. It has a rough side and a smooth, shiny side, and it is always best to lay the board shiny side up. Make sure that the hardboard is stored in the room it is to be laid in for a few days before you actually secure it in place. This allows it to acclimatize to the atmospheric conditions of the room.

1 Butt the edges of the hardboard sheets up against each other, and either nail them to the floorboards or use a staple gun, as shown here. Stagger the joints and secure each board along the edges and every 6–8 in (15–20 cm) in all directions.

2 To fit, score the sheets using a craft knife and straightedge—a spirit level is ideal because the shaft of the knife can be rested against the spirit level as it is drawn along the cutting guideline. The knife will not cut all the way through the sheets.

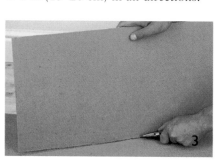

3 Turn the board over and fold it upward so that it snaps along the scored line. Use the craft knife to finally cut through the board on the opposite side of the scored line. Position the cut piece of board and nail or staple it in place.

LAYING PARTICLEBOARD

Particleboard is thicker than hardboard and is generally used to make floor surfaces in new homes, rather than using traditional floorboards. It can be used over old floorboards to provide a flat, level surface, but its most common use is to provide a solid subfloor for carpets or vinyl flooring.

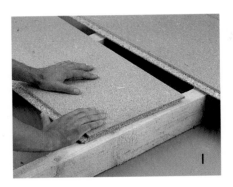
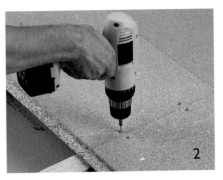

1 Particleboard has a tongue-and-groove jointing system which means that each new board edge is fitted into the previous one in order to make a strong flush joint.

2 It can be fixed to the joists with nails, but screws make a more solid fixing and reduce the risk of loosening with age. Stagger the board edges and cut them so that they join on a joist and not in between them.

3

LAYING PLYWOOD

Plywood is another building board that has many general uses, including being used as a subfloor in some situations. Where hard tiles or block flooring are to be laid, it is important to ensure that there is little or no flexibility in the subfloor. Laying plywood on top of the existing floor, whether it be traditional floorboards or particleboard, reduces flexibility and provides a sound surface.

Attaching plywood: for a subfloor, the sheets of plywood should be about ¾ in (18 mm) thick. They can be either screwed or nailed down, and as with all forms of subfloor, the edges should be staggered.

PAINTING FLOORS

O ne of the most straightforward methods of refurbishing a floor is to paint it, but this is only possible if the surface has been well prepared. Floorboards, subfloors, and concrete floors can all be revitalized by being painted.

FLOORBOARDS

Floorboards should be sanded to remove the previous coatings (see pages 46–47). Once prepared and cleaned, they can be painted to produce a hardwearing surface that is easy to keep clean. It is always advisable to use proprietary floor paints since they tend to be the most durable, although gloss paint and some all-purpose water-based paints, which should be coated with varnish to give a final protective layer, can also be used.

1 Prime the floorboards before paint application, to ensure that the surface is sealed and to provide a good base for the subsequent coats of floor paint.

2 Apply the floor paint, brushing with the grain of the boards. Use a generous amount of paint on the brush and brush the paint into the surface, making sure that it does not "pool" in any areas. Two coats of paint should be sufficient for most floors, although hallways and other areas that have a lot of wear and tear may need more coats.

The grained look: instead of priming and applying each coat of paint all over the floor, simply paint each floorboard and then wipe away the excess paint with a cotton rag as you proceed across the floor. In this way, the grain of the wood is exposed, to give a timber-rubbed effect, which offers an alternative to the opaque finish of most painted floors.

PAINTING SUBFLOORS

It is possible to paint subfloors, as long as you have made sure that the surface is totally clean and free from dust and particle debris. Prime the floor surface first to make sure that it is sealed, as this will give the best possible top coat adhesion. Because of their relatively flat surface, subfloors offer the opportunity to paint intricate designs and patterns that would be difficult to carry out on any other floor surface. The example here shows how to paint a border stripe—simple to do and very effective.

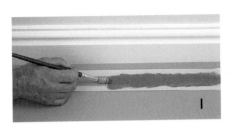
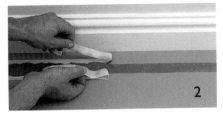

1 Paint the floor its base color and let dry. Apply two strips of tape around the edge of the room, 1 in (2.5 cm) apart. Paint between the strips with a contrasting color.

2 While the paint is still wet, pull away the masking tape strips to reveal a contrasting stripe bordering the entire room.

3

CONCRETE FLOORS

Concrete floors are not common inside the home but there is sometimes a storage room that has no other floorcovering than bare concrete. Garages and basements are also areas where there may be a concrete floor. Painting these floors can add a touch of "finishing," while reducing dust and making the floors easier to keep clean. However, you should not paint new concrete screeds until you are sure they are totally dry; this may take weeks or even months—always use a moisture meter to check the floor before painting it.

1 Sweep the floor thoroughly, then remove any grease spots or impurities from the floor with a proprietary solvent.

2 Apply floor paint directly onto the concrete— some manufacturers may recommend thinning the first coat slightly in order to seal the surface, although this will not be necessary in most cases. A roller covers the floor quickly, then a brush may be used to finish off around the edges.

LAYING LAMINATED FLOORING

W ood stripped floors are difficult to lay, but it is now possible to create the same effect by using laminated flooring, which mimics the effect of its more traditional counterpart. Laminated floors tend to be laid as a "floating" floor, so called because the individual boards are not stuck directly to the subfloor below. Instead they are laid on a foam underlay that adds acoustic and thermal insulation to the floor, as well as leveling out any rough areas on the subfloor. The latter point is particularly important when laying laminated floors on concrete screeds that are not totally smooth. Overall, the "floating" floor system makes this surface very easy to lay and combines interlocking tongue-and-groove boards with adhesive to create a hardwearing and easy-to-clean floorcovering.

3

1 Roll out the foam underlay onto the subfloor surface. Make sure that it is totally flat with no folds or kinks in it, and that its edge is butted up against the baseboard. The underlay can be cut quite easily with scissors or a craft knife in order to fit it where required.

2 Lay the sheets of laminated flooring on the underlay and against the baseboard, inserting wedges along its edge. These wedges, which are usually supplied with the flooring as part of the kit, ensure an expansion gap for the entire floor. Make sure that they are all inserted to the same level.

3 To join the next sheet of flooring, run some adhesive along the tongue of the previous sheet. Lock the groove of the new sheet over this tongue to join them together. Make sure that the ends of the boards are staggered as you build up each new row of sheets.

4 To ensure a tight joint, use a hammer and block to knock each laminated sheet firmly in place. If no block is supplied with the flooring, use a scrap piece of laminate. Never directly hammer the edge of the sheet or you will damage it.

5 Wipe away the excess adhesive that is squeezed out of the joint with a clean rag. Make sure that this is done immediately, before it has a chance to dry. Continue to build up sheets, row by row, across the floor until the surface is completely covered. At some stage you will need to cut some boards to finish off along the edges. This can be done with an ordinary handsaw. Once the floor is completely covered, remove the wedges and use some quadrant beading to cover the floor/baseboard junction.

4

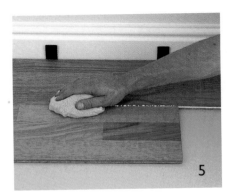

5

3

LAMINATED FLOOR CONSIDERATIONS

Laminated floors are relatively easy to fit, but there are a few considerations that need to be taken into account before you decide to lay them.
- Suitable areas: laminated floors are suitable for most areas in the home, except those places which are prone to damp or rooms with a high amount of moisture. Bathrooms, for instance, are not ideal for this type of flooring.
- Concrete floors: as long as the floor is old and well established, there is no problem in laying a laminated floor on a concrete surface.

However, new screeds must have dried totally before a laminated floor can be laid on them. Test the moisture content of a new screed with a moisture meter to ensure that it has dried before you start.
- Covering edges: the expansion gap around the edge of a laminated floor can be covered with some quadrant beading as suggested in Step 5, above. However, a neater alternative is to remove the baseboard before the floor is fitted, then you can replace it afterward and it will cover the expansion gaps.

PREPARING FOR FLOOR TILING

L aying tiles or parquet-block flooring requires a certain amount of planning to ensure that the desired finish is achieved. Although these types of flooring are laid in different ways, there are certain similarities in the way the application layouts are planned and the measures that need to be taken to prepare the floor prior to application.

PLANNING

It is difficult to use the edge of the room as a "square" guideline for starting, since most rooms do not have precisely square corners or walls. To lay any type of tile or block flooring, you need to find the center of the room and plan the layout from this point. This way it is possible to centralize any design and ensure that cuts around the perimeter of the room are balanced. The diagram below demonstrates the best method for planning the layout for a floor-tiling project.

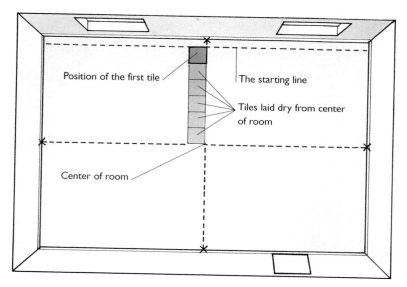

Position of the first tile

The starting line

Tiles laid dry from center of room

Center of room

To find the center of the room, mark off the midpoint of each wall, and hammer a small nail into the floor at this position. Attach a chalk-line string between opposite nails and snap the string to create a chalk impression on the floor. Where the two lines bisect will be the center of the room. These lines can then be drawn over with a pencil to make them more distinct.

The position of the starting line will depend on the tile dimensions. It should be measured back from the central point of the room, using tiles laid dry to find out where the best tile positions will fall.

LEVELING FLOORS

For wooden floors, it is essential to have a flat, rigid surface before tiles may be laid. They should be prepared as shown on pages 50–51. For concrete floors that are rough or uneven, it will be necessary to level off the screed by using a self-leveling compound. Before applying the compound, ensure that the screed is totally clean and free from any impurities. Some manufacturers suggest using a proprietary floor sealant before applying the compound.

1 Mix the compound to a thick liquid consistency according to the manufacturer's guidelines (this is usually a simple case of adding water to powder). Pour the compound onto the floor, allowing it to spread across the concrete surface.

2 Use a plaster float to spread the compound across the floor surface. Gradually it will begin to find its own level, gathering more in depressions in the floor and less at the high points. Allow it to dry thoroughly before beginning to tile.

ESTIMATING QUANTITIES

Before beginning a tiling job, it is important to work out what the material requirements are. This is a case of simple arithmetic.
- Estimating tiles: multiply the wall dimensions of the room together to provide a surface area, then divide this by the size of one tile. This gives an exact quantity requirement. Add 10–15 percent to this figure to allow for cutting and breakages, and also to have a few spare tiles at the end of the job to allow for repairing any damaged tiles in the future.
- Estimating adhesive: often the manufacturers are slightly mean when it comes to recommending how much adhesive is required for a particular area—always buy more than the suggested amount to ensure that you will have enough to complete the job.

CAUTION

Always make sure that concrete floors have dried thoroughly before tile application. In most cases, it will be necessary to apply a proprietary sealant to the floor before you can start tiling it.

3

WOOD-BASED TILES

C ork and parquet panels are attractive floorcoverings, providing relatively hardwearing surfaces that are easy to clean. Traditional parquet floors are made from individual wooden blocks; today, there are tile-size panels available that are easier to lay.

LAYING CORK TILES

Make sure that cork tiles are laid out dry in the room to be tiled for two to three days before application, so that they can become accustomed to the atmospheric conditions of the room. Find the center of the room (see page 56) and measure back to one of the farthest walls to find the best starting point, then draw in the starting line, as required. Only apply adhesive to an area of the floor large enough for a working period of about 20 minutes at a time.

1 Apply adhesive to the floor using a notched spreader. Leave it for 30 minutes until it is "tacky." Apply the first tile at the junction between the starting line and the bisecting room line.

2 Continue to lay tiles, butt-joining the edges. Cork tiles can be cut, as required, using a craft knife and a straightedge. Fit cut tiles around the edge of the room, as needed.

3 Once quite a few of the tiles have been laid, use a rolling pin across the tile surfaces to ensure that they are all well bedded into the adhesive and that they are level.

FINISHING THE FLOOR

Some cork tiles have a prefinished surface, and they require no extra treatment once laid. However, in other cases, it will be necessary to seal the surface once it has dried, using the varnish or sealant that the manufacturer recommends. No preparation is required, it is simply brushed onto the cork tiles.

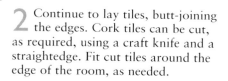

LAYING PARQUET PANELS

As with all wooden floorcoverings, parquet panels should be allowed to acclimatize to the atmospheric conditions within the room before they are laid. The period of time should be weeks rather than days, if possible, because the jointing system of parquet panels requires time to adjust completely before they are fixed in place.

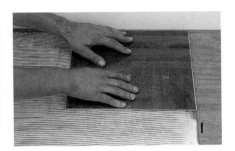

1 If the room dimensions allow for it, and the wall adjacent to the starting line (see page 56) is relatively square, begin laying panels along a starting line that is the width of the cork expansion strips away from the wall (see below). This distance is usually ½ in (12 mm). As with cork tiles, allow the adhesive to go "tacky" before applying the panels.

2 Parquet panels are joined using an interlocking tongue-and-groove system. Build up the rows of panels until the floor is complete. Using an ordinary handsaw, cut panels to fit the edges, as required. Finish around the edge of the whole room, next to the wall, by inserting cork expansion strips.

3 Cover the expansion strips by nailing a piece of quadrant beading around the floor perimeter. Secure it in place by knocking in brads through the quadrant and into the baseboard. The quadrant can then be stained to match the floor finish, or painted to match the baseboards. Alternatively, remove the baseboards before applying the panels, then replace them afterward, covering the cork expansion strips.

CORK EXPANSION STRIPS

Flexible cork expansion strips are a necessary requirement for parquet panel floors. They absorb any slight movement by the floor panels.

HARD-TILE FLOORING

H ard tiles are the most durable of floorcoverings. They are supplied in various forms and finishes—the most common are ceramic floor tiles. Some of the alternative hard tiles are more difficult to lay, but, once you have achieved a good basic technique for laying ceramic tiles, the other options become much easier.

LAYING CERAMIC FLOOR TILES

Ceramic floor tiles must be laid on a level surface, whether it be concrete or a wooden subfloor. Use the planning diagram on page 56 to find the center of the room and to work out the best position for the starting line. You can nail a wooden batten along the edge of the starting line to provide a solid edge to butt the first row of tiles up against, though this is not absolutely necessary.

1 Apply tile adhesive to the floor using a large notched spreader. Position the first tile at the junction between the starting line and the room bisecting line. As you move the tile into position, twist it slightly to ensure good adhesion.

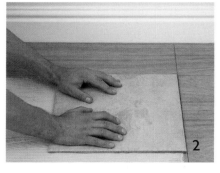

2 As you build up the tile design, position spacers between the tiles to maintain a consistent gap for grouting later on. Continue to add rows of tiles until all the full tiles in the room are laid.

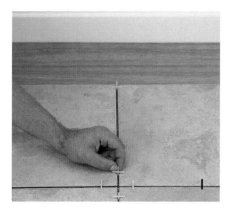

3 Allow the adhesive under the full tiles to dry before filling in around the edges with cut tiles. Standard tile cutters can be used to cut most floor tiles. If you have a lot of cuts to make, it may be worthwhile renting a machine cutter; follow the manufacturer's instructions for use.

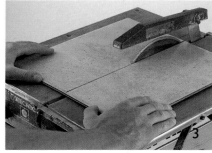

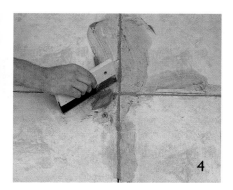

4 Once the entire floor has dried, remove all the spacers, then grout the joints between the tiles. Be sure to use floor grout rather than wall-tile grout because it is more durable. Press it into all the joints with a grout spreader.

5 Before it sets, wipe away excess grout with a damp sponge. Once the floor is completely grouted and the grout has set, polish the surface of the tiles two or three times with a dry cotton rag to remove any "cloudy" residue left by the grout.

ALTERNATIVE HARD TILES

The following types of hard tiles require a slightly different technique for laying.

- Quarry tiles: these tiles are often smaller than ceramic floor tiles but they are slightly thicker. Instead of laying them on ordinary tile adhesive, they should be laid on a bed of mortar. For this reason, it is best to divide the floor into sections, separated by wooden battens, so that the mortar bed and the quarry tiles can be kept level. Most types of quarry tiles will need machine cutting for edging purposes.

- Flagstones: although not technically a tile, flagstones tend to fall into this category of hard flooring. Like quarry tiles, they need to be laid on a bed of mortar, and mortar is also used to grout them, rather

than the usual floor-tiling grout. Flagstones are very heavy and can be unusual shapes, which makes them a difficult flooring to lay.

- Marble tiles: to a certain extent, marble tiles can be treated like ordinary ceramic tiles, but the grouting spaces between the tiles should be reduced so that they create the effect of a continuous marble floor.

- Slate and natural stone tiles: most of these types of tiles can be laid like ceramic tiles, although care is needed to protect their surface until they are grouted and sealed. Slate, especially, is easily ingrained with grout residue and dust unless its surface is well sealed with a proprietary sealant.

CARPETING FLOORS

C arpet still remains one of the most popular floorcoverings, due to its comfort factor. There are many different types with varying qualities to choose from. Most carpets are either burlap-backed or foam-backed. Burlap-backed carpets tend to be better quality, but are more difficult to lay. Foam-backed carpets, which are often less expensive, can be very hardwearing. They also have the advantage of being relatively simple to lay.

FIXING THE EDGE

The way the carpet edges are dealt with is one of the main differences between laying burlap-backed or foam-backed carpets. Both types of carpet need to be secured around the perimeter of the room, but the methods by which this is achieved are very different.

Foam-backed carpets: the foam backing of these carpets means that the harsh structure of a "gripper rod" cannot be used to hold it in place. The best way to secure it is simply by using double-sided carpet tape. Stick this around the edge of the room and peel away the top layer before sticking the trimmed carpet in place. Carpet joints in central areas of the room may also be secured with double-sided tape.

Burlap-backed carpets: this type of carpet requires "gripper rods" to be positioned around the edge of the room. The carpet is then stretched over and behind the rods in order to hold it taut and in position. The metal teeth on the gripper rods dig into the carpet's burlap backing and hold it tightly in position. The gripper rods are attached to the floor by simply hammering in nails along its length—for concrete floors, use masonry nails. It is a good idea to hold a piece of scrap board by the baseboard to prevent it from being knocked by the hammer while the gripper rods are installed.

STRETCHING CARPET TO FIT

Burlap-backed carpets need the help of a carpet stretcher to ensure that they are held tautly in position. Underlay is usually laid across the floor surface first because this increases the insulation and the comfort factor of the carpet. Underlay should be rolled out, butt-joined at the edges, and trimmed where it reaches the gripper rods. Do not allow it to encroach onto the gripper rods.

1 Cut the burlap-backed carpet into the baseboard/floor junction using a craft knife. Be careful not to cut into the baseboard. It does not matter if the cut is not totally accurate since the carpet fitting process is not yet complete.

2 Using the carpet stretcher, work outward from the center of the room to the edges, ensuring that the carpet is stretched out and perfectly flat. Hold the carpet with the gripping end of the carpet stretcher, while using your knee to knock against the broad pad at the base of the stretcher to force the carpet toward the edge of the room.

3 Use a brick chisel to force the edge of the carpet over and behind the gripper rods around the edge of the room. Again, be careful not to damage the baseboard—just use the broad face of the chisel to mold the carpet into position.

Entrances: finishing carpets at doors or other room entrances is always a problem. The easiest way is to attach a threshold strip, which acts in the same way as a gripper rod, securing the carpet in place. The type you use will depend on the floorcovering in the next room. Here, a chrome edge provides a boundary between the carpet and a wood-planked floor.

LAYING VINYL FLOORING

I n many ways, vinyl flooring crosses the boundary between hard-tile floors and carpets. Although it has a hardwearing surface that can be wiped easily, it also provides a cushioned effect underfoot, which is lacking with hard-tile floors. These qualities make vinyl flooring a popular choice for kitchens and bathrooms. It can be laid on concrete screeds or wooden subfloors. Ideally, it should only be stuck down around the edges and along the joins. Vinyl is difficult to install because there is none of the tolerance that carpet has in terms of stretching and positioning. Therefore, measurements and cuts must be that much more precise. The best way of installing vinyl flooring is to first make a paper template that exactly replicates the size of the room in which the vinyl is being laid.

1 Attach the template to the full vinyl sheet with tape. Make sure that the pattern on the vinyl sheet and the edge of the template are adjusted so that they will produce the best possible position for a balanced pattern once the flooring is laid. Trim around the template using a craft knife, leaving a 3-in (7.5-cm) excess all around to allow for final trimming while positioning.

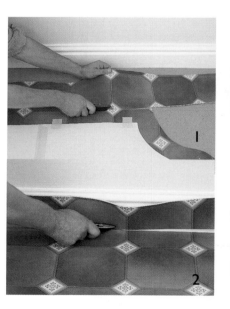

2 Position the vinyl sheet, creasing its edge into the corner junctions. Trim away the excess by cutting directly into the baseboard/floor junction with a craft knife. Cut the vinyl sheet slightly above the junction in each case, to allow for any unevenness along the edge.

3 The edges of the vinyl sheet can be secured in position with double-sided tape or adhesive. In large rooms, it may be necessary to join sheets; in which case, try and use the factory edges, rather than cutting the joint yourself. These areas will also need securing with double-sided tape or adhesive to stop them from lifting away from the floor.

Intelligent Storage

4

INTELLIGENT STORAGE

Most of us are constantly trying to make more space in our homes and reduce the everyday clutter. It is therefore important to devise storage systems around the home that can counteract the clutter and produce a sense of order. Storage systems vary in size and specific function, which makes them an interesting area of home improvement. This chapter shows you how to find creative solutions for particular storage problems and demonstrates innovative ways to make these systems attractive as well as practical. In addition to standard storage solutions, there are many ideas for transforming existing systems into interesting and attractive storage areas.

4

UNDERSTAIRS STORAGE

T he area under the stairs is often a much underused part of the home and one that is worthwhile considering for refurbishment. In some cases, it may be possible to turn the area into a downstairs bathroom, although some professional help will be required to carry out a project of this nature. More often, understairs areas can be turned into useful storage space.

Closed system: a neat, compact finish can be achieved by constructing a closed system that encloses the entire understairs area. This makes good use of the space while maintaining an understated look. The design of such systems will vary according to the available space and the general layout, but a simple construction is usually the best.

4

THE TRADITIONAL LOOK

For a traditional look, a paneled storage system with hinged doors is a good way of integrating it into the rest of the decorative scheme.

Sliding compartments: instead of using traditional cabinet doors, a more innovative approach is to create sliding compartments that bring the storage system out into the hallway when access is required. It makes access to the shelves much easier, but it does require more advanced skills to create such a storage facility.

4

Open system: rather than closing off the storage area below stairs, it can be just as practical—and very attractive—to keep it open and create a more visible storage system with easy access to all the things kept there.

Display system: in some situations, it may be better to use the area under the stairs as an open storage and display system. The actual size of the whole system and the depth of the shelves will depend on the design of the staircase.

WINDOW SEATS

W indow seats can be constructed to form an excellent storage
system while providing an attractive feature in your home.
They are best suited to windows with a relatively deep recess to give
enough depth for a reasonable seating area.

SEAT CONSTRUCTION

The design, size, and depth of window recesses may vary dramatically, but
there are a number of general principles that apply to the construction of all
window seats. The most important consideration is to ensure that the seat is
hinged so that it can be opened to provide valuable storage space.

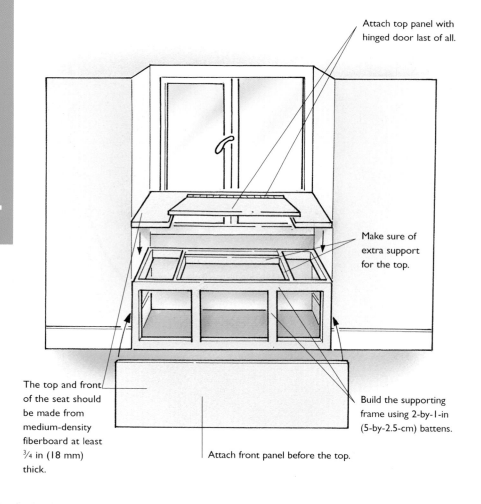

Attach top panel with
hinged door last of all.

Make sure of
extra support
for the top.

The top and front
of the seat should
be made from
medium-density
fiberboard at least
¾ in (18 mm)
thick.

Attach front panel before the top.

Build the supporting
frame using 2-by-1-in
(5-by-2.5-cm) battens.

ATTACHING THE HINGE TO THE SEAT

The trickiest part of building a window seat is creating the hinged door to allow access to the storage area underneath the seat. The easiest method is to cut the actual door out of the top surface of the seat using a jigsaw. The cut-out portion can then be turned into a door by attaching a flush hinge all the way along its length before reattaching it to the main seat area.

1 Cut the flush hinge to the length of the medium-density-fiberboard door with a hacksaw. Position the hinge along the edge of the door, reverse side upward. Mark with a pencil the position of each screw point along the length of the hinge.

2 Remove the hinge. Then drill pilot holes at every pencil mark along the edge of the door.

3 Position the hinge the right side up and screw it in place, ensuring that it fits flush along the edge of the door. To fit the door to the main part of the seat, again drill pilot holes, then secure in place with screws.

4

A WINDOW SEAT

Window seats combine practicality and good looks to produce an excellent feature in any room. The tongue-and-groove paneling across the front of this seat is given a stylish look by the sumptuous cushions arranged along the top of the seat.

USING THE CEILING

T he ceiling is often a neglected area when it comes to considering storage systems. However, as long as it is possible to secure firm fixings, all sorts of suspended shelving and racking systems can be created to give practical and attractive storage areas.

CHOOSING A STYLE

Ceiling storage is usually a hanging system—a modern version of the old-fashioned clothes airing rack. This basic design is the ideal way of storing all manner of items, while keeping them easily accessible for everyday use, and it has become a popular way of storing cooking utensils in the kitchen.

Integrating the scheme: painting a hanging rack the same color as the kitchen cabinets helps to integrate the rack into the overall scheme and create a well-balanced and coordinated look.

4

Utilizing space: racks suspended from the ceiling are a perfect way of using space that would otherwise be wasted. They also avoid cramping any of the open, uncluttered areas in a kitchen.

HANGING A CEILING RACK

It is essential to have secure ceiling fixings that can take a substantial weight when hanging this type of storage system. Fixings should always be made in the ceiling joists to ensure a solid base. Most racks require four hooks and it can be tricky to find enough fixing points that correspond with the precise place where you want the rack to hang. There may have to be a compromise between the ideal hanging place and the ideal fixing points, in order to hang the rack securely.

1

2

1 Measure from the ceiling/wall junction and mark the ideal position for one of the fixings.

2 Use a joist detector to find out if there is a solid joist at the marked point. If there isn't one, find where the nearest joist is (and therefore the position of a suitable fixing point). From this fixing point, the remaining fixing points can be planned—joists always run parallel to each other so finding further points becomes progressively easier.

3

3 Drill a pilot hole in the joist before screwing the hook into position. A screwdriver acts as a useful lever to make screwing in the hook much easier.

CAUTION

When drilling into the ceiling, make sure that there are no supply pipes or wires in the area where you are drilling, otherwise you risk damaging them and possibly injuring yourself.

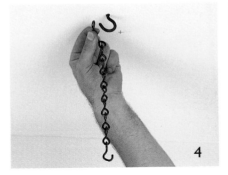

4

4 Attach a chain to the hook, then find the next fixing point and insert another hook. Continue to add fixings, as required, and then hang the rack in position.

CABINETS

C abinets provide an essential part of the storage capacity in most homes. They are an important area of concern when remodeling and improving your home. Making the best of cabinet capacity and its appearance is therefore important when considering storage.

Cabinet styles: the term "cabinet" is used to refer to all sorts of sectioned-off storage spaces around the house. Choosing the best system for a particular area is very important for creating the right balance between being functional and looking decorative in a room.

Closets: these can be separate items of furniture or they can be fitted into the overall scheme of a room. The latter option saves space by making use of alcoves and other redundant areas. Decorating the closets so that they become integrated into the room's color scheme can also be very effective.

4

Cabinet combinations: storage facilities do not have to be confined to one system—one attractive option is to combine closed-off cabinets with more open storage areas, such as these open shelves.

Display cabinets: one of the more decorative aspects of a storage system is the facility to combine the two functions of storing and displaying items at the same time. A glass-fronted cabinet, filled with pretty items like glass or china, can do this with impressive effect.

CHANGING A CABINET'S APPEARANCE

Many cabinets can have their entire appearance transformed by changing
the doors, or by simply altering the look of the existing ones. The method
by which this is achieved will vary according to the design of the cabinet.
The examples shown here demonstrate how a simple panel door can be
dramatically changed using one of several decorative finishes.

Removing the middle: to change the
look of a panel door, first remove the
central area, so that an alternative
decoration can be attached to the
door. On some designs the panel will
fall out with a few firm hammer
knocks; in other cases, it may be
necessary to cut out the middle panel
using a jigsaw. Drill four holes, one
at each corner of the central panel, to
accommodate the jigsaw blade and
allow for accurate cutting.

The mirror look: use mirror adhesive to stick
a mirror to the back of the door frame. For a
heavy mirror, use special mirror fixings. You
can change a single door in this way, or a
number of doors as part of an overall fitted
closet system—the effect can be quite dramatic.
Ensure that the mirror you choose is
appropriate for door use and is shatterproof.

4

The material look: attach wire mesh and fabric
to the back of the door frame to give the front
a rustic look. Pull the mesh and fabric taut and
secure in place with a staple gun.

Using fretwork: cut a piece of fretwork the size
of the door and paint it a contrasting color
to the door frame. Pin it in place on the back
of the frame. This produces an attractive open
display system for a cabinet.

SHELVING 1: INCREASING HEIGHT

S helving is probably the most common storage system found in our homes. Shelves benefit from a makeover just as much as any other household fixture. One way of revamping a shelving system is to give it a different look by creating the illusion of greater height.

USING FLAT STRIPS

One of the easiest ways of giving shelving the illusion of greater height, or a more solid look in general, is to pin flat strips of lipping along the front edge of the shelves. Calculate how much lipping you require by simply measuring the combined lengths of the shelves you wish to remodel.

4

1 Cut the lipping to size and hammer in some brads along its edge before positioning it against the shelf. It is much easier to start hammering brads into the lipping while it is off the shelf, rather than trying to do it when it is in position.

2 Hold the lipping against the edge of the shelf and hammer the brads into the shelf, making sure the top edge of the lipping is flush with the surface of the shelf. Use a nail punch to ensure that the brad heads go in below the surface level.

3 Use all-purpose filler to fill the brad-head holes. Leave it to dry before sanding the entire edge to a smooth finish.

4 Paint the shelf, then give the edge an added decorative effect by stamping a design along it—this will also enhance the more solid appearance the shelving now has.

USING A DECORATIVE MOLDING

A similar "height increasing" effect can be achieved by using a more decorative molding to act as the front edge to the shelf. This in itself provides greater opportunity for extravagant decorative paint effects, transforming the original simple shelving system to a far more eye-catching and creative feature.

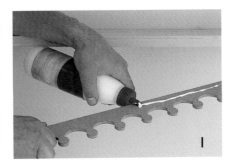

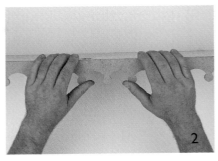

1 As an alternative to using brads to secure the molding in place, it is possible to use wood glue. Glue is especially suitable if the molding is lightweight and unlikely to slip once it has been positioned and the glue is drying.

2 Position the molding, ensuring that its top edge is flush with the broad surface of the shelf.

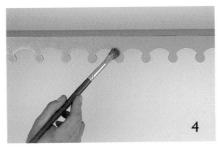

3 Once the glue has dried, paint the shelf and molding to blend both components together and make them into a more solid-looking single shelf structure.

4 Gold highlighting is a good way to add decorative interest to the shelf front. Use a fine paintbrush with very little gold paint on the bristles—ensure that the excess paint is removed after you have loaded the brush. Gently brush backward and forward across the edges of the molding to produce a highlighting effect which gives an aged, antiqued appearance to the whole shelf.

SHELVING 2: ALTERNATIVE IDEAS

O ne of the most satisfying aspects of home improvement is coming up with original ideas or developing techniques and finishes to suit your own particular preferences. These sentiments can be applied to shelving just as much as to other areas of the home—there is a great sense of fulfillment to be derived from this kind of personal endeavor.

ALTERNATIVE DECORATIVE EDGES

Attaching moldings is one way of increasing the dimensions of a shelf (see pages 74–75), but you can also use color and a range of other materials to give a greater decorative impact to a shelving system. All kinds of things can be used for this process—the items shown below are just a few examples.

Upholstery studs: adding upholstery studs creates a very solid edge along a shelf. This is enhanced by painting the shelf base a rusty red color to complement the metallic finish of the studs. The studs can be positioned in a neat row, as shown, or in a meandering line for a more random effect.

4

Fabric trim: trim or decorative braid makes a very attractive edging for a shelf. Use double-sided tape to secure the trim or braid in place.

Door moldings: moldings designed specifically for door panels can also be fixed along the edge of a shelf to give it decorative appeal. Painting the molding a different color than the main shelf will add a pleasant contrast. Secure the molding in place with double-sided tape.

USING FABRIC

Fabric is not usually associated with shelf construction and in many cases it would be considered inappropriate. However, fabric can be used to great effect for covering shelves and creates a very different look. Choose fabric that complements or contrasts with the rest of the decoration in the room. This technique is best used for shelves that are not fixed in place since they must be taken down to be covered.

1 Treat the shelf as if you were gift-wrapping it. Cut the fabric accordingly, so that the dimensions will cover both sides of the shelf while leaving an excess at each end.

2 Fold one side of the material over and onto the top of the shelf. Apply some self-adhesive hook-and-loop tape along this fabric edge, but do not allow the tape to come into contact with the shelf surface itself.

3 Apply the corresponding side of the hook-and-loop tape to the other edge of the fabric, folding the edge of the material to make it neat. Now fold the fabric over and onto the shelf surface, joining the hook-and-loop tape to create a bond.

3

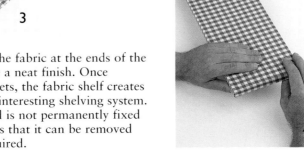

4 Finally, fold in the fabric at the ends of the shelf to produce a neat finish. Once positioned on brackets, the fabric shelf creates a very unusual and interesting shelving system. Because the material is not permanently fixed to the shelf, it means that it can be removed and washed, as required.

SHELVING 3: LOOKING AT OPTIONS

S helving is usually confined to wide open areas of wall space, because that appears to be the most obvious or easiest position for it. However, if you want to be more inventive about shelving, you can produce all kinds of novel systems, all of which can add an extra dimension to the appearance and function of your shelving.

4

UTILIZING SPACE

The secret of utilizing space is to create shelving in areas that would otherwise be redundant. This has the effect of producing an interesting decorative feature, while satisfying practical needs. The following are a few examples of areas where shelving can be built to give this sort of effect.
- Fireplaces: disused fireplaces provide an ideal area for shelving in what would otherwise be wasted space.
- Picture rails: create a shelf at picture-rail height to make use of otherwise unused wall space.
- Dado trim: as with picture rails, the area directly above dado trim is often unused. In many cases this is because a shelf would stop furniture from being placed against the wall. However, where this is not the case, a dado-level shelf is a serious option for creating extra storage.
- Radiator shelf: positioning a shelf above a radiator can help to draw the eye away from the radiator itself. Always leave a gap between the radiator and the shelf to allow the air to circulate. Also, make sure that the shelf is made from a board such as medium-density fiberboard— softwood shelving is likely to warp with the heat from the radiator.

- Above doors: this is another under-used area that can be enlivened by the addition of a single shelf.
- Valance: the frame of a window valance can often make a useful ornamental shelf as long as it is made from a material that is substantial enough to be load-bearing.
- Corners: building a shelving system across a corner can provide a useful storage area, as well as smoothing the angular appearance of a corner and giving a better decorative effect.
- Integral shelving: not all shelving has to be for display—there is often a lot of wasted space in the larger storage systems, such as cabinets and closets. Adding shelves to the underutilized spaces in these areas can provide a great deal of hidden storage capacity.
- Bathrooms: because bathrooms are one of the smaller rooms in the home, space-saving ideas are essential. Rather than store toiletries outside a shower cubicle, have a storage facility in the shower for items that will not be affected by moisture. Manufacturers are very innovative in this area and they are producing lots of designs for shower shelving and hanging systems.

WINDOW SHELVING

This may appear to be an unlikely area to consider when thinking about shelving, but not all windows have a breathtaking view or let in a great deal of light. In such cases, it can be worthwhile using the window for a shelving system, creating an attractive and useful area in what was otherwise a rather bland and underused area of the room.

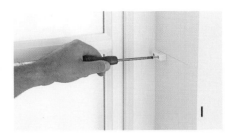

1 Draw a level pencil guideline in one side of the window recess at the height where you want the shelf to be positioned. Screw in two jointing blocks along the pencil guideline to act as the shelf supports.

2 Cut the shelf to size and rest one end on the jointing blocks. Pencil a guideline on the opposite side of the recess, using a level to ensure that it is straight. Secure two more jointing blocks and position the shelf.

4

ORIGINAL SHELVING SYSTEM
This pretty window shelf combines practicality with a very original look. The ornamental and display properties of this type of shelving are highly effective.

BOTTLE RACKS

Custom-made storage systems are a good way of ensuring that they can fulfill a specific function. Whatever the system, it is always more rewarding if it is as attractive and innovative as possible. In this example, old clay drainage pipes have been used to make a bottle rack.

1

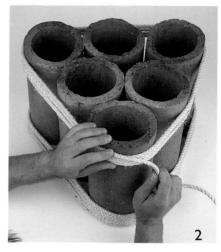

2

4

1 Position the lengths of pipe so that they form the shape of a triangle. Make sure that they are tightly packed together.

2 Use some fairly coarse rope to bind around the perimeter of the pipe arrangement. Keep each new loop around the pipes taut and positioned adjacent to the previous loop. The most effective final design is to have a grouping of loops at what will be the back of the rack and a similar-size grouping at the front.

THE RUSTIC LOOK
The finished rack provides a perfectly functional and very attractive storage system for most types of bottles. The natural finish of this sort of pipe blends well with all kinds of textured surfaces, such as an old slate floor or a textured plaster wall finish.

Finishing Touches

5

FINISHING
TOUCHES

The smaller finishing touches in an overall refurbishment can often make the largest impact, so this area of remodeling is just as important as the larger constructional projects. Choosing the correct fixing mechanisms for these finer details can sometimes be tricky, so this chapter provides precise instructions for a variety of finishing touches and effects to enhance the look of your home. Remember that most finishing touches are best chosen once a room has been redecorated, when most of the furniture and fixtures are back in position. In this way, it is easier to make decisions about the position of pictures, for example, or whether a paper border is needed to add a final touch of color and decoration to the look of the room.

5

PICTURE HANGING

Most people have a variety of pictures in their homes. The size of the picture, the type of frame, and the place where you want to hang it will all influence the way it is hung on the wall. It is therefore important to choose the right fixing and to attach it to the wall using the correct technique. Although there are some revolutionary designs in this area, which can be helpful in certain situations, the traditional methods are usually more than adequate.

GROUPING PICTURES

Hanging single pictures is usually a straightforward case of holding the picture in the desired position, marking the spot on the wall, and inserting a hook, as required. However, the process is slightly more demanding if a number of pictures are used to form an arrangement, or specific grouping, as shown in this example.

1 Once the first picture is in position, the remaining ones can be measured from this point. Hooks will go into most wall surfaces if you use a hammer to knock them into place.

5

2 Use a level and a tape measure to position the next hook, adjusting your calculation to account for the picture size, whether you are using an even or a staggered design, and how many pictures are going to be in the final grouping. Continue to position hooks until the required amount are inserted into the wall.

A GROUPED IMPRESSION
A group of pictures that are all the same size gives a decorative and well-ordered finishing touch to a room.

USING FLUSH FIXINGS

In some cases, it may be necessary to hang a picture so that it sits flush and secure against the wall surface. This is usually the case in corridors or any areas where the picture may be easily knocked; standard hooks would allow the picture to be moved out of place, or possibly even damaged.

Fixing in place: the best attachments to use for pictures that need to sit flush are glass plate fixings. These flat plates are screwed to the back of the picture and then the remaining hole houses the screw that fixes the plate (and therefore picture) to the wall, as shown. The number of plate fixings required will vary according to the size of the picture.

HEAVY PICTURES

Standard picture hooks are fairly robust, but with heavier pictures you may want the added peace of mind gained from using more substantial fixing mechanisms. There is no simpler method than using a straightforward wall anchor and long screw. As well as the fixing, make sure that the string or wire on the picture itself is strong enough to take its weight.

1

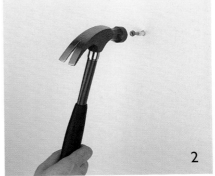

2

5

1 Drill into the wall surface at the required position in order to make a hole for the screw fixing. Hold the drill at a slight angle so that the screwhead, when inserted, will be pointing ceiling-ward slightly.

2 Knock in the appropriate size anchor and screw with a hammer, before screwing into position with a power driver. Leave enough screwhead showing to loop the picture wire over it. Make sure that the screwhead is large enough to hold the picture wire on the screw.

MIRROR HANGING

A lthough mirrors are generally hung on the wall like pictures, their hanging system varies slightly from the more traditional hook mechanisms. It is preferable to have the mirror secured flush against the wall surface, so that its reflective qualities can be used to the best possible advantage.

FLUSH FIXINGS

There are a number of types of flush fixings available, and indeed in some cases the glass plate fixings shown on page 83 can be used. However, one of the best methods to attach a plain mirror securely on the wall is to use the flush fixing-brackets shown here.

1 Hold the mirror in the required position on the wall, making sure that the mirror is precisely level, then draw a light pencil guideline around its edge. Once the guideline is drawn, put the mirror to one side.

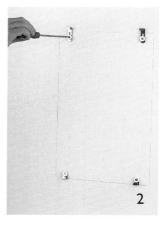

2

2 Screw four flush fixing-brackets into the wall, two along the bottom edge of the guideline and two along the top edge. The bottom brackets are designed to fit rigidly in one position; the top ones can move slightly.

5

3

3 Fit the bottom edge of the mirror into the two lower brackets and push it flat against the wall. The sliding mechanism on the top two brackets allows them to sit higher than the edge of the pencil guideline until after the mirror is inserted. It is then possible to slide these upper brackets over the top edge of the mirror and secure it firmly in place.

HIDDEN FIXINGS

Where a mirror has predrilled holes, it is possible to use a different type of discreet fixing mechanism—mirror screws. These differ slightly from the standard screw fixing in that they have a threaded hole that runs down the central shaft of the screw. This is used to house a chrome cover cap, which hides what would otherwise be an unattractive finishing detail on the mirror.

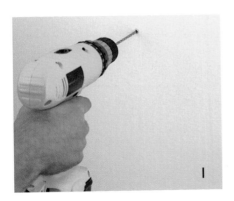

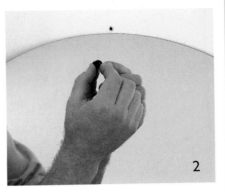

1 Mark and drill the required number of holes for the mirror, using a drill bit that corresponds to the size of the mirror screws you are using.

2 Mirror screws come supplied with rubber rings, which should be positioned in the mirror holes on the reflective side. These help to prevent the mirror from cracking as the screw is driven into place.

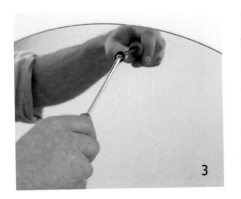

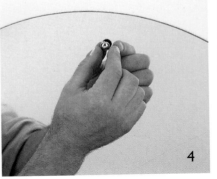

3 Drive the mirror screw into place, being careful not to overtighten it. Apply just enough turns to ensure a secure fixing, allowing the screwhead to nestle inside the rubber ring.

4 Screw the chrome cover cap into the head of the mirror screw to cover the screw and provide a more attractive fixing. Apply more mirror screws and caps to other holes in the mirror, as required.

5

HANGING TEXTILES

R ugs, throws, and textiles in general provide a particular problem when they are being hung on the wall because they do not have a rigid structure and cannot be treated in the same way as pictures or mirrors. In order to display such items in a way that will show them to full effect, they should be hung using the methods shown here.

USING GRIPPER RODS

In most cases, carpets are placed on the floor, but they can be displayed on the wall, making an attractive feature in a room. Gripper rods can be used to hold the carpet in position, but should not be used for valuable antique carpets.

2 Attach the edge of the rug to the gripper rod, pressing it into position along the serrated edge of the rod. Be careful not to scratch your fingers when positioning the rug as the gripper rod teeth can be very sharp.

1 Cut a gripper rod to the precise width of the rug you want to hang. Nail it into the wall at the appropriate height, using a level to make sure that it is straight.

5

COMBINED DISPLAY
A combination of pictures and textiles across a wall surface provides a dramatic and impressive wall display.

USING A DOWEL

In some cases, it is possible to hang a rug using a piece of wooden dowel. This method can only be used when the rug has looped tassels, so that the dowel can be threaded through them and then hung on the wall to hold the rug in position.

| Cut a length of dowel to the width of the rug and carefully thread it through all the tassels on the end of the rug. Insert two hooks in the wall, slightly less than the width of the dowel apart, and position the dowel in the hooks.

UNUSUAL FEATURE
Rugs and carpets like this one, usually found on the floor, make an extremely attractive feature when they are hung on the wall.

HANGING A THROW

The flimsy nature of a throw means that it needs a larger number of fixing points to keep the material taut and in a good position to display it properly. The exact number of fixing points will vary according to its size.

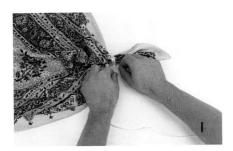

1 Take each corner of the throw and use some nylon thread to bind around the material, making a securely tied-off section.

2 Position hooks on the wall, and loop the nylon thread over the hooks, adjusting the material, as necessary, to produce the best effect.

HOOKS AND PEGS

H ouseholds can never have enough hooks and pegs for hanging up all manner of everyday clothing. However, they are often forgotten until the rest of the room has been redecorated. In many ways, this is an advantage because you can then position them where they will be useful but still incorporated into the decorative scheme.

MAKING PEGS

Pegs are an attractive hanging system that can add a pleasing finishing touch to a room, as well as being practical. Use a 5-by-1-in (12.5-by-2.5-cm) plank as the base for the pegs and some simple wooden dowel for the pegs themselves.

1 Cut a piece of 5-by-1-in (12.5-by-2.5-cm) planking to the length you require for the base. Draw a pencil guideline centrally along its length. Make a further series of guidelines bisecting the central one at equidistant intervals along its length. Each bisection of the central line represents the position of a peg.

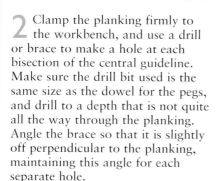

2 Clamp the planking firmly to the workbench, and use a drill or brace to make a hole at each bisection of the central guideline. Make sure the drill bit used is the same size as the dowel for the pegs, and drill to a depth that is not quite all the way through the planking. Angle the brace so that it is slightly off perpendicular to the planking, maintaining this angle for each separate hole.

5

3 Cut the required number of dowel pegs. Apply a generous amount of wood glue to the pegs and insert them into the drilled holes. Wipe away the excess glue once they are positioned. Leave to dry. The rack can be painted before or after it is fixed to the wall. For a natural wood finish, rub out the guidelines before applying stain and/or varnish.

USING HOOKS

As with pegs, hooks tend to look best if they are mounted on a wooden base before they are fixed to the wall. Softwood planking can be used (see opposite); alternatively, a length of hardwood, as shown here, makes an excellent base that contrasts well with the metallic finish of the hooks themselves. To maintain the decorative appeal of this storage system, the fixings used to position the hardwood base on the wall can be hidden behind the hooks, giving a neat and attractive finish.

1 Cut a piece of 5-by-1-in (12.5-by-2.5-cm) hardwood planking to the length required. Place the hooks at equal distances along its length. Lay a tape measure along the wood; mark the screw holes for the hooks.

2 Drill a series of pilot holes in the hardwood at each pencil mark, making sure that the drill goes into the surface of the wood vertically.

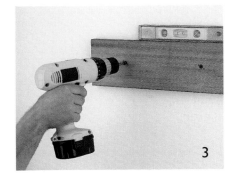

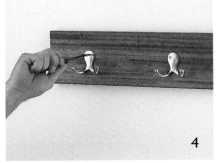

5

3 Position the wooden base on the wall using a level, and drill fixings between the pilot holes for each of the hooks. Screw the base firmly in position on the wall. Then, before proceeding, oil the wood to give it a good finish.

4 Finally, screw the metal hooks in place, covering the fixings that are holding the wooden base securely on the wall.

FRAMING

G iving some sort of decorative frame to an item in a room can provide a lively finishing touch that helps to integrate everything into the decorative scheme and also adds extra interest to particular features in the room. Framing can be done in a number of ways, from hand-painted designs to masked-off areas that are painted to provide a solid color frame. In the examples shown here, different techniques are used to produce borders that act as an additional frame.

SPONGING A FRAME

A sponged frame can be painted around a picture on the wall. Use colors for the frame that complement those used in the picture itself.

1 Mask off a border around the picture on the wall, then use a natural sea sponge to gently dab paint inside the masked-off area.

2 Carefully remove the masking tape to reveal a neat sponged frame around the picture.

5

Stamping: use a stamp to apply a themed border around the edge of the picture. Position the stamp by eye to give a random finish.

Stenciling: buy or make your own stencil border design to add a frame to the picture. Be careful to realign the stencil each time it is moved.

MAKING PAPER BORDERS

As an alternative to paint, a paper border makes an attractive decorative frame around a feature in the room. Such borders are more commonly used at dado or ceiling level, but they can be very effective when used as a framing mechanism, as shown here. Because mitered or right-angled turns are required for this technique, try and choose a border with a busy pattern so that these corners will appear to be matched correctly. A window provides an excellent area to use this framing technique.

1 Apply lengths of border so that they overlap completely at the corner of the window recess. Try to adjust the lengths so that the overlap runs through the busiest part of the pattern—this will be cut through to provide the mitered join.

2 Hold a straightedge (a level is ideal), so that it runs through the corner. Use a craft knife to cut very carefully and evenly along this line, through the overlapping lengths of border paper.

3 Gently peel back the two lengths of border paper and remove the excess strips of paper that have been cut free from the main part of each length.

4 Reposition the end of each length to produce a perfect mitered butt-joint. Always remember to wipe away any excess adhesive with a damp sponge before it dries.

LIGHTING

L ighting is one of the major elements for creating atmosphere and mood in a room, so it is important not to overlook it when you carry out any sort of makeover. Try to assess the practical needs of the room in terms of its lighting, before exploring your own ideas on the kind of light effects you wish to achieve. Always consult a qualified electrician if any rewiring work is required for the type of lighting you want to install.

Downlighting: ceiling downlighters always provide excellent light for work areas and also produce good overall lighting for any room. Some spotlights are fixed, but it is possible to install "eyeball" types, which can be moved in their sockets to provide an alternative direction for the light. Combining spotlights with other directional lighting above the table adds to the atmosphere created by the lighting in this room.

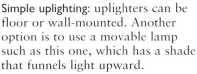

Simple uplighting: uplighters can be floor or wall-mounted. Another option is to use a movable lamp such as this one, which has a shade that funnels light upward.

5

Traditional lamps: these are the most versatile of all lighting systems since the shade can be changed to give a new look, and they can be moved around the room to create a different ambiance. Height is an important factor when positioning a lamp— low-level lighting produces a more intimate, cosy atmosphere than a light source at a higher level.

Quick Fixes

QUICK FIXES

Remodeling certain areas in the home may simply be a matter of fixing something that is damaged, altering existing fixtures to change their style, or some general redecoration that quickly and effectively gives a room a new look. This chapter covers all these areas, as well as giving advice on overcoming and repairing damaged surfaces, general maintenance, and the best way to keep your home functioning efficiently. In addition to providing the solutions for all kinds of problems, there are lots of ideas on style and how to achieve a particular look. Many of the projects provide a quick and easy way of carrying out a refurbishment, but it is still important to use the most efficient methods, so that there is no compromise between quality of finish and the time it takes to complete the job properly.

REPAIRING WALLS

D amage to solid block walls can be repaired with filler or plaster. Stud walls are made from drywall attached to a framework. If they are damaged, it exposes a hollow cavity. As filler or plaster will simply fall into the cavity, an alternative repair method is required.

FILLING SMALL HOLES

Small holes in drywall can be repaired by a simple patching process where filler is applied to the hole, but only after a solid drywall base has been fitted to the inside of the cavity to prevent the filler from falling into it.

1 Use a craft knife to trim away any loose areas of drywall from the edge of the hole and make a neat surface. Cut a small piece of drywall that is slightly larger than the dimensions of the hole once it has been straightened and trimmed.

2 Drill a small hole in the cut piece of drywall and thread some string through it, knotting it on one side. Apply some glue around the edge of the piece on the other side to the knot. Drop it through the hole in the wall, holding onto the string to prevent the piece from dropping into the cavity.

3 Use the string to pull the piece of drywall onto the back of the hole. While the adhesive is drying, secure the piece in position by tying the string to a scrap of wood positioned flush against the wall.

4 Once dry, remove the scrap of wood and cut off the string. Use all-purpose filler to fill the hole, secure in the knowledge that the drywall patch will prevent the filler from falling into the cavity.

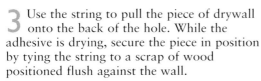

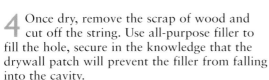

LARGE HOLES

More severe damage in drywall requires an alternative method to achieve a sound repair and finish. For any damaged areas larger than about the size of a small envelope, the following method should be used.

1 Use a craft knife to mark out a rectangular area which incorporates the hole and extends as far as the wooden vertical wall supports on each side of the hole.

2 Depending on the thickness of the drywall, use a craft knife or saw to trim back the guidelines neatly to the wooden supports. Make sure that there are no hidden cables or pipes in the wall cavity that you could damage during this process. Ensure that the vertical edges of the area run precisely down the middle of the vertical wooden supports. Remove any nails from the exposed area of wood.

3 Cut a piece of drywall to a size fractionally less than the dimensions of the rectangular hole. Position the piece of drywall and secure it in place by nailing along the vertical junctions with the existing plasterboard wall.

4 Mix up some one-coat plaster to a smooth but stodgy consistency. Apply the plaster to the "patch" using a plastering float. Keep returning to the patch as it dries, smoothing the surface with the plastering float until a good finish is achieved.

6

REPLACING TILES

Replacing tiles is an effective way of changing the look of a room, but it can be a time-consuming operation. Fortunately, there are options other than full replacement of the tiles—it is possible to give a tiled surface a different look by adding some extra decoration. Also, if some of the tiles on a surface are damaged, individual tiles can be replaced, rather than have to retile the whole area. If you do decide to retile, remember that as long as the old tiles are stuck down firmly, they can be used as a base for the new tiles. This will save a lot of preparation time and speed up the project quite considerably.

TILING MAKEOVERS

If retiling is not an option, it is possible to refurbish existing tiles and create a totally different look with any of the following ideas.

- Borders: adding border tiles to an existing design can have the effect of revitalizing the whole surface. There are various options when choosing borders—even using full tiles of a contrasting color will provide a fresh looking finish.
- Paint: old tiles can be painted as long as they are prepared properly. Use either a tile primer or a proprietary surface preparation compound on the tiles before applying any coats of paint.
- Reviving grout: many tiled surfaces are let down, not by the look of the tiles themselves, but by the poor condition of the grout between the tiles. Use a grout raker to remove the old grout before regrouting the whole tiled surface. Since it is possible to buy grout in different colors, you can use it to make a decorative contrast with the tiles.
- Replacing caulking: caulking acts as a waterproof seal around tiled areas.

However, it will deteriorate over time. Cutting out the old seal and replacing with new, will give a neater and brighter finish. Alternatively, a decorative wooden molding can be used as a seal. Paint it first and position it using caulking.
- Stencils and stamps: revive an old tiled surface by using stencils or stamps to paint designs onto the tiles. Use ceramic paints and then varnish the painted tiles. This design technique is not ideal for areas where there is a lot moisture, such as shower cubicles or backsplashes.
- Transfers: tile transfers can be used in a similar way to stencils, to add a picture or design to individual tiles. As with stencils, transfers are not ideal for use on tiles that suffer regular water attack.
- Adding picture tiles: remove a few of the old tiles from the surface (see opposite for the technique) and substitute them with picture tiles.
- Change a backsplash: rather than retiling the entire area, simply tiling a new backsplash can revitalize the look of the whole tiled surface.

6

REPLACING A SINGLE TILE

Despite their tough glazed surface, tiles do get damaged and then they spoil the look of the entire tiled surface. Rather than total tile replacement, it is a relatively straightforward job to remove a damaged tile and fix a new one in its place. It is always a good idea after any tiling project to keep the leftover tiles for just such a circumstance—it can be very difficult to match the colors and shades of new tiles to an older surface.

1 Drill some holes in the damaged tile to weaken its surface before you try to remove it. Do not drill too close to the edges of the tile or you risk damaging the surrounding ones. Use a tile drill bit first, to break the glazed surface of the tile. Change to a larger masonry bit to increase the size of the hole, if necessary.

2 Wearing goggles to protect your eyes and using a hammer and brick chisel, remove the old tile, being careful not to damage the surrounding area. Make sure that all tile fragments are removed from the wall surface.

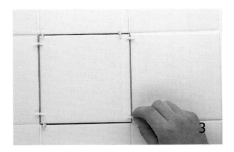

3 Apply tile adhesive to the back of a new tile and position the tile in the hole. Use spacers, fitting them perpendicular to the tiled surface in order to maintain the gap for grout and prevent the tile from slipping out of position before the adhesive is dry.

4 When the adhesive has dried, remove all the spacers. Mix some grout to a smooth, creamy consistency and work it into the gaps using a grout spreader. Remove any excess grout from the tiled surface before it sets, using a damp sponge.

6

REPAIRING FLOORBOARDS

W here the general condition of floorboards is poor, the best option is total replacement. However, in many cases it is possible to repair damaged areas by cutting out the old boards and replacing them with new ones. The technique varies according to whether the boards have flat edges or a tongue-and-groove design.

FLAT-EDGED FLOORBOARDS

These floorboards are simply planks of wood used to cover the floor joists. Replacing a damaged part of one of these boards is quite straightforward.

1 Use a brick chisel to lever up the damaged area of board. In this example, the split begins at the end of the board; however, even if the damage is more central to the board length, it is best to begin by lifting the board at one end.

2 Place a length of batten under the damaged area of board to hold it up above the floor. Saw through the board at a point where it is no longer damaged and is above a floor joist.

3 Remove the damaged section of floorboard, then hammer the end of the undamaged section of board back in position.

4 Cut a new length of board the same size as the damaged section of board. Hammer the new section in place at the joist.

6

TONGUE-AND-GROOVE BOARDS

This design of floorboard requires a slightly different technique when it comes to replacement. Because the edge of each board locks into the adjacent one, it is not possible to simply lever up a board at the end, as shown, with flat-edged boards. It is necessary to free the edges before the board can be removed.

Cutting the tongue: in order to remove a tongue-and-groove board, use a saw to cut through the board tongue. Allow the saw blade to run down the edge of the board, but be careful not to damage any wires or supply pipes that may be below floor level. Once the board edges are cut, follow Steps 1–4 opposite—it is difficult to use a tongue-and-groove board as a replacement so, in this case, use a flat-edged board instead.

FLOORBOARD PROBLEMS

Aside from the more extensive damage that floorboards can experience, there are a number of minor problems that can be overcome with relative ease. There are also a few extra tasks that can be carried out when floorboards are replaced, in order to help things like the decoration and the general look of the floor.

- Squeaky boards: the remedy can be a simple case of screwing or nailing down any loose boards. However, in many cases, these may not be very obvious, but a generous sprinkling of talcum powder along board edges and joints often solves the problem of squeaking boards.
- Dealing with gaps: on a decorative level and in terms of drafts, gaps between floorboards can cause a problem. Use thin wedges of wood to fill these areas and plane them until they are flush with the floor surface. If the floor is going to be

covered, the look is not important and you can use a wood filler to fill the gaps before laying the new floorcovering on top.

- Using the access: if floorboards do have to be taken up, draw a plan of the pipe and wire network below floor level. This knowledge will be useful for knowing where cuts can and cannot be made for any future refurbishing projects.
- Like for like: where a damaged board is in the center of an exposed floor area, replacing it with a new board will result in the repair standing out against the surrounding floor and this will spoil the overall look. In cases like this, take up an old, but sound, board from under an item of furniture or a rug and use this to make the repair. A new board can then be used to patch the area below the furniture or rug where it will not be seen.

6

REPAIRING BASEBOARDS

B aseboards provide the most basic decorative trim for most rooms in the home, and if they are to show off the room to best advantage, they need to be in good condition. Therefore, repairing any damaged sections of baseboard is an essential home improvement task during a refurbishment. The technique required to repair a baseboard depends on whether it is minor or major damage.

SMALL HOLES

Minor damage in baseboards, such as small nicks, scrapes, and gouges, all of which are the result of everyday wear and tear in the home, can be simply filled with an all-purpose filler, then sanded back to a smooth finish before the baseboard is repainted. For slightly larger holes, it is advisable to use a different technique to ensure that the repair will be a long-lasting one. Such repairs are needed when fixtures are removed from a baseboard position or, as shown in the example below, some pipes have been rerouted, leaving unsightly holes in the baseboard.

1 Mix some proprietary wood filler and press it firmly into the holes. Wood filler is much harder than all-purpose filler and does not shrink when applied in areas such as this. Because it dries to such a hard finish, make sure that the filler does not sit higher than the holes, as it can be a lengthy process to sand it back.

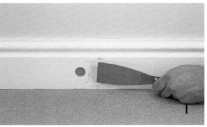

2 Once it has dried, use some fine-grade abrasive paper to remove any excess filler from the baseboard surface and provide it with a key for the next step.

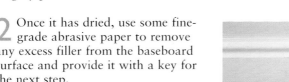

3 Apply a thin skim of fine surface filler over the holes to give the best possible finish. Leave the filler to dry, then sand again with fine-grade abrasive paper before painting.

6

LARGE HOLES

For large holes in a baseboard, or areas that are damaged beyond a simple filling repair, some form of replacement will be necessary. While it is possible to cut out sections of baseboard, this can be a difficult and very time-consuming process. It is much easier to replace the entire length of baseboard. Unless the baseboard is particularly ornate, it is relatively inexpensive to buy and, by using a new length along a wall, the finish is certain to be much better than trying to camouflage a patched area.

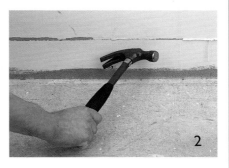

1 Use a hammer and brick chisel to prise the baseboard away from the wall. Try not to damage the wall area above the baseboard while carrying out this process.

2 Remove any old nails from the baseboard area, otherwise these will interfere with the new length once it is attached. A new section can now be cut and secured; if lengths need to be joined, it will be necessary to follow Steps 3 and 4, below.

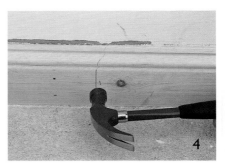

3 If you need to join lengths of baseboard, miter the joining end of the new length and secure it to the wall. Apply some wood glue to the cut end of the length.

4 Attach the next length, and join it to the first board, having measured and cut the opposite miter so that the two pieces fit together. Hammer in small nails or brads to make the joint secure and prevent it from splitting open at a later date.

6

INTEGRATING A DOORMAT

A small but very effective home improvement can be achieved by integrating a doormat into the carpet by the front door. Not only does it create a better finish than simply having a separate mat, it can also be cut to the exact size you require. Although the mat will give the appearance of being fixed in place, it will still be possible to remove it for periodic cleaning. The example shown here is for a carpeted floor, but the technique can easily be adapted for wooden or tiled floors by simply following the basic principles of the procedure.

1 Measure the required area for the mat, using a piece of chalk to mark the carpet in the required places. The precise design will vary according to taste, although a straight edge usually gives the best finish. For a slight variation, the corner areas can be cut across the angle to add some extra interest to the final mat shape.

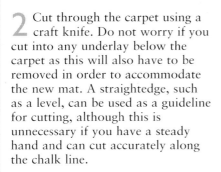

2 Cut through the carpet using a craft knife. Do not worry if you cut into any underlay below the carpet as this will also have to be removed in order to accommodate the new mat. A straightedge, such as a level, can be used as a guideline for cutting, although this is unnecessary if you have a steady hand and can cut accurately along the chalk line.

3 Remove the excess piece of carpet and underlay, then use a hacksaw to cut a section of carpet-edging strip to correspond with the length of the cut carpet edge. If you have an angle or corner in the mat design, it will be necessary to join sections of the strip with mitered joints. Nail the strip in position precisely along the cut edge of the carpet and underlay.

6

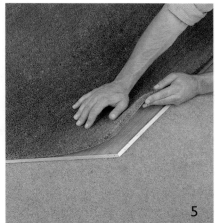

4 Use a brick chisel to feed the edge of the carpet into the serrated edge of the carpet-edging strip. Make sure that there are no hollow areas under the carpet, as any bumps or dips will ruin the whole effect—it is important to force the carpet edge firmly into the carpet-edging strip.

5 Finally, cut some core matting to the size of the hole and fit it into the hole, making sure that its edge is tightly butted against the carpet strip. Depending on the type of mat, it can either be cut using scissors or a craft knife. With some matting, it may be worthwhile making a template for cutting, in order to achieve a neat finish.

THE INTEGRATED FINISH
Installing a built-in mat by the front door provides a practical and attractive way of stopping mud and dirt from being trailed through the rest of the house.

6

KITCHEN FIXES

Totally redesigning a kitchen is a major operation that most people carry out on a very infrequent basis. When it comes to remodeling the kitchen, it is a matter of finding alternative ways of changing its look without incurring a heavy work load and major expense.

SIMPLE TECHNIQUES FOR CHANGE

Making changes to kitchen cabinets is a very simple process because most of them are designed along similar lines at the basic level; therefore, changing one component for another is usually a relatively straightforward operation.

REVAMPING OPTIONS

There are many options for remodeling the look of a kitchen. Using one or more of the following ideas will help to change its overall look and improve the practical facilities.

- Cabinet fronts: most kitchen cabinets are constructed of carcass base units that are of a very similar size and dimension, only varying according to their specific function—in other words, a wall cabinet base unit made by one manufacturer is very similar to one produced by another. The more decorative aspect of the kitchen is achieved by the actual doors and drawer fronts that are attached to these units. Therefore, the appearance of the entire kitchen can be changed by replacing existing unit fronts with new ones. When choosing this option, always check that the new fronts will fit the older base units—sometimes some slight adjustments need to be made to make them fit accurately.
- Painting cabinets: instead of replacing cabinet fronts, it is possible to paint them instead. The exact method of achieving this will depend on the actual surface of the cabinets. If the

cabinet has a non-wooden surface, it will be necessary to use a proprietary surface preparation compound to ensure that the surface will accept coats of paint.
- Changing a countertop: in spite of their hardwearing properties, countertops tend to be the areas that wear out the fastest in the kitchen and this detracts from the smart look of the room. Replacement can be a tricky job, especially if there are a number of joints in the countertop surface or the sink is cut into it. One option is to tile the countertop, eliminating the need for the more extensive task of completely replacing the units. Furthermore, the tiling can be extended to cover the old tiles above the countertop and produce a more complete makeover.
- Lighting: in any room, the lighting has a great effect on its mood and atmosphere. By experimenting and changing the source of directional lighting, or by simply adding to the existing arrangement of lights, you can produce a completely different feel in the room.

6

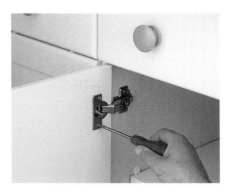

Replacing doors: most kitchen cabinet doors are hinged in a similar way and are simple enough to unscrew and change for a different design. In most cases, it is possible to use the existing hinge on the base unit to secure the new door.

Changing door hardware: this is usually secured with a single threaded bar or screw that extends from the handle side of the door through to the interior side. Changing the handle on a cabinet is a simple case of unscrewing the old one and changing it for the new one.

Changing a plinth: plinths on kitchen cabinets tend to be secured in place with a clip-on bracket system. It is easy to pull the old plinth away and replace it with a newer design or finish.

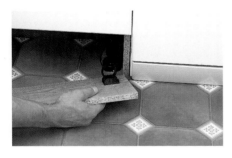

THE MADEOVER LOOK
Simple remodeling in an old kitchen, such as changing handles or painting cabinets, can breathe new life into it, altering its appearance and extending its overall life span.

6

DECORATING 1: LARGER SURFACES

D ecorating, which is a major part of any refurbishment, can be carried out on a large scale to totally change the look of the room or it can be a matter of paying attention to specific areas that need some attention. The largest surfaces in most rooms tend to be the walls and ceiling, and there are many ways in which a makeover can transform these areas independently of other surfaces in the room.

PAINTING WALLS

The options for painting walls are extensive, whether it be a simple color change or a more adventurous move toward paint effects and textured finishes. Opting for a change of color or style can be a quick but effective way of achieving a transformation.

PAINTING OPTIONS

- Touching up: in many cases the only repainting that is required for a refurbishment is touching up the existing scheme with the same color. Where possible, use the original can of paint that was used to paint the walls to cover up any scrapes or marks on the wall—a new paint of the same color may be from a different batch in the manufacturing process and a slight change in shade may show up on the wall surface. In such cases, paint the entire wall with the new paint, cutting in precisely along the corners—although the change would be noticeable when two slight shade differences are shown on one wall, it will not be noticeable if the color variation is between separate walls.
- Masking: if you are using a roller, mask off the baseboard to prevent paint spray from getting on the wooden surface, otherwise you may have to paint the woodwork.

- Color-washing: this simple paint effect is a quick and easy way of changing the look of the wall. Use the existing wall color as a base coat and dilute some emulsion with water, or use some colored glaze to apply a wash on the wall surface.
- General effects: there are various other paint effects that can be used to brighten up an existing scheme—sponging and ragging are generally the simplest options. These can produce more dramatic finishes—although any paint effect will result in a marked difference from the existing scheme.
- Adding designs: stencils and stamps are ideal for adding a decorative edge to an existing color scheme. They can both be used to create a pattern or a border. Stencils and stamps can be bought very cheaply. Alternatively, if you want to produce a more individual look, you can make your own.

6

PAPERING WALLS

The alternative to refurbishing walls with paint is to use wallpaper instead. Completely papering a room can be a relatively large decorating project, since it may be necessary to extensively prepare a smooth wall suface first. However, there are a number of ways in which wallpaper can be used in a more selective manner to change the look of wall surfaces in a room.

PAPERING OPTIONS

- Adding borders: applying decorative paper borders to walls is a simple way of changing the look of a room. Borders are made in all sizes and depths so you can choose according to your personal preference. There are also options as to where on the wall to apply the border—it can be used at ceiling level to provide an attractive decorative edge, or at dado trim level to divide the wall area into two parts and create a more interesting look.

- Single walls: rather than wallpapering the entire room, you can paper a single wall to make it more of a feature in the room.

- Making panels: wallpaper panels make an attractive feature on wall surfaces, especially if the chosen paper has a very distinct or heavily patterned design. This idea looks particularly impressive above dado trim. Each panel can be framed with a border to provide further effect.

- Paneling wood: wallpaper may also be used to cover the natural panels found on doors or cabinet fronts. This is a good way of coordinating the wall design with the woodwork.

- Adding texture: a textured paper on a wall is a good way of covering up rough wall surfaces, as the embossed texture of the paper will disguise it.

- Lining: although lining paper is used as the preparatory paper layer for some wallpapers, it can also be used as a wallcovering in its own right. Although it will not even out the surface of rough walls like an embossed paper will, it certainly makes a smoother surface which accepts paint exceptionally well.

- Part paper: instead of wallpapering the entire wall surface in a room, paper up to dado level, dividing the wall space into two decorative effects. Draw a level pencil line around the perimeter of the wall at dado height, then hang paper up to this pencil line. Cover the edge with a border to give it a neat finish.

- Keeping clean: after wallpaper has been applied, it is important to wipe excess paste and adhesive off surfaces, before it dries.

- Extending life span: a coat of acrylic varnish can be applied to uncoated papers to protect the surface and

6

DECORATING 2: WOOD AND OTHER SURFACES

O nce the wide-open wall spaces in a room have been decorated, it is time to consider the smaller areas such as the woodwork. In fact, these details often form an essential part of any makeover, providing the finishing touches to a color scheme.

DEALING WITH WOOD

Wood is found in most rooms in the form of baseboard and various frames, doors, and cabinet fronts. Whatever they are used for, wooden surfaces need to be refurbished from time to time to keep the room looking in good condition and stylish.

WOOD OPTIONS

- Touching up: touching up small nicks or scrapes in woodwork with the original color can help to restore a piece of wood to good condition. However, in many cases, it is worth painting an entire section or area, rather than wasting time looking for small scrapes and minor damage to touch up. If a length of the baseboard has areas that need recoating, for example, it is usually just as quick and more effective to paint the entire length, rather than just the damaged parts.
- The focal points: instead of painting all the woodwork in a room, simply paint the focal points and larger

surfaces, such as doors and windows, as this will help revitalize the color scheme.
- Natural wood finishes: wood that has been coated with varnish or stain needs reviving after a while. Applying a coat of the appropriate finish from time to time will help keep these areas looking good.
- Using paint effects: in a similar manner to walls, woodwork can be revitalized using paint effects. The techniques that look the best tend to be the textured finishes, such as dragging and graining. Use acrylic glaze to create these effects.
- Highlighting: picking out features on wooden surfaces with a different color can add extra interest. On a panel door, for example, it can be extremely effective to paint the moldings that make up the edges of the panels a different color than the main area of the door. Or, paint window sills a contrasting color to the window frames.

6

OTHER SURFACES

In addition to wood, which makes up many areas in most rooms, there are any number of miscellaneous surfaces that require retouching from time to time. Whether metallic or constructed from man-made compounds, most of these surfaces can be painted to give them a general overhaul and a more attractive appearance. The secret of painting such surfaces successfully is knowing what is required in terms of preparation and what paint should be used to achieve the best finish.

MISCELLANEOUS SURFACES

- Radiators: these are very easy to paint as long as a few simple rules are followed. Make sure that the radiator is turned off while painting. If there are no visible rust spots on the surface, there is no need to apply any primer. Two coats of eggshell paint, or one each of undercoat and gloss paints, is the best procedure. As a design feature, radiators are not the most attractive of objects, so it is worth considering painting them the same color as the wall, so that they blend in rather than stand out from the wall. After all, not all refurbishment is aimed at making a statement, and in this case camouflaging the radiator can be the most effective form of improvement.
- Window hardware: this is often a neglected area of decoration, and the entire look of a window can be let down if the window hardware is covered in splashes of old paint, or has simply discolored. Brass or iron-effect window hardware should be left the natural color, but other metals and alloys can be painted successfully. Unscrew them from their position on the window, and place them on an old board before using an aerosol paint to spray them the color of your choice. Allow them to dry completely before repositioning them. This technique can also be used on various types of door hardware as well.
- Glass: windows, and any other glass areas, are ideal for revamping with paint. Use proprietary glass paints for this. Creating your own stained glass effect, or a hand-painted design, can produce a novel finish.
- Laminates: many modern surfaces in the home have a laminated finish, which is hardwearing and easily cleaned. Kitchen cabinets, for example, often have a laminated finish. These finishes must be properly prepared before paint can be applied to them. A proprietary preparation compound must be used and then coats of paint can be applied in the usual way.
- Fireplaces: revamping a fireplace with paint often depends on whether the fireplace is active or not. If inactive, the mantel, hearth, and grate can all be painted with ordinary household paints. However, if the fireplace is in regular use, heat-resistant paints must be used. The mantel shelf and its supports can usually be painted with standard paints as they do not come in close enough contact with high heat. If in any doubt, always consult a professional for advice on the correct paint to use for your particular situation.

6

HOME MAINTENANCE

O ne of the most important aspects of home improvement is ensuring that your house is well maintained and that all the services and warning systems are working. Many of the areas of concern are listed below, with suggestions for how to check them.

HOME CHECKLIST

- Water meters: it usually becomes apparent very quickly when there is a water leak in the home, but outside the home this can be less obvious. A monthly check of your water meter to see how many units are being used will soon show if there might be a leak between the main water-supply pipe and where it enters your home.

- Electrics: the fuses in the electrical wiring system act as the warning for any problems with outlets or appliances. Most electricity suppliers offer a free electrical check service and advice on whether any wiring should be updated or renewed.

- Gas: any problems with gas become apparent very quickly because of its smell. Never take any chances with gas, and if you do detect a leak, call your local supplier immediately. All gas appliances should be regularly maintained. Central heating systems should be serviced once or twice a year, depending on the make. Read the installation and instruction manuals for all your gas appliances to check when they need servicing. Never try to service appliances yourself—always use a professional.

- Security alarms: intruder alarms are becoming a very popular addition to most homes, and it is important that they function properly so that they can do their job should the need ever arise. The maintenance of such systems varies, but most are very simple and quick to check. Use your operation manual for guidelines.

- Smoke alarms: these are one of the simplest yet most effective safety mechanisms and are essential in every household. Battery-operated alarms tend to have an alert noise if the battery is running low. As a further safety check, they can be tested manually with a button that will set off the alarm briefly to make sure that it is working. Don't take risks—check alarms weekly.

- Carbon monoxide alarms: because carbon monoxide has no aroma, high levels in the home cannot be detected by smell. Special alarms have been developed to solve this problem. Most are electrically operated, and it is important to pay particular attention to the manufacturer's guidelines on where they should be installed in the home. As with smoke detectors, the alarm can be tested manually with a button that will set off the alarm briefly to check that it is working correctly.

SIMPLE MAINTENANCE

Many household problems can be avoided by following simple maintenance guidelines. Some have already been discussed on the opposite page, but the examples below show other areas where general maintenance can help to prevent problems from occurring at a later date.

MAINTENANCE GUIDELINES

- Lubrication: it is always a good idea to keep your water supply valves well lubricated. Then if you have to turn off the water in an area of the home, or for the whole house, the water supply valve will turn easily. Proprietary aerosol lubricants are best for this purpose. This method of lubrication can also be applied to household locks, to ensure they remain in good working order.
- Drainage systems: make sure that all the drains and the flow of waste out of the house is an efficiently functioning system. Use a proprietary drain cleaner from time to time to keep the waste pipes in good working order.
- Gutters and downspouts: these areas must keep water flowing, otherwise blockages and drips can cause damp problems on internal walls. Make sure that the gutters are cleared seasonally to ensure that water flow is always maintained.
- General cleaning: on a decorative level, painted and papered surfaces will deteriorate much faster if they are not kept clean. This also applies to floorcoverings. Regular cleaning will increase the life span of all these surfaces in the home.

EMERGENCIES

However vigilant you are about maintenance in your home, from time to time it may be necessary to deal with an emergency, and it is important to have some sort of action plan to deal with such occasions. The following checklist provides excellent guidance, showing you the best way to be prepared for any unwelcome emergencies.

EMERGENCY CHECKLIST

- Telephone numbers: keep a list of emergency telephone numbers in a safe place that is known to all the household members. As well as emergency services, this list should contain numbers for professional plumbers and electricians.
- Supply switches and valves: stay aware of the places where all the household supply systems can be turned off in an emergency.
- Escape routes: make sure that the household is able to deal with fire emergencies and that escape routes are kept clear. Your local fire safety officer can provide advice on the particular needs of your home and any necessary improvements.

6

INDEX

A
alarms 26, 110
attics, insulation 24, 25

B
baseboards 30-1
  repairing 100-1
bathrooms 78
battens 32, 33
blanket insulation 25
bolts, door 17
borders, paper 91
bottle racks 80
burglar alarms 26, 110

C
cabinets 72-3, 104
carbon monoxide alarms
  26, 110
carpets 62-3
casement windows 15,
  16
ceilings
  coves 34-5
  plaster roses 37
  storage systems 70-1
ceramic floor tiles 60-1
chains, door 17
closets 72
concrete floors, painting
  53
cork expansion strips 59
cork tiles 58
corners, baseboard, 30
countertops 104
coves 34-5
curtain fixtures 18-21

D
dado trim 28-9, 78
display cabinets 72
doors
  cabinets 73
  door furniture 12-13
  doormats 102-3
  double glazing 23
  finishing carpets at 63
  flush doors 40-1
  insulation 24
  kitchen cabinets 105
  problems 39
  security fixtures 17
  shelving above 78
  styles 38

double glazing 22-3
dowels, hanging textiles
  87
draft eliminators 24, 25
drywall, repairing 94-5

E
electric fireplaces 43
electricity supply 110
emergencies 111

F
fabric
  cabinet doors 73
  on shelving 77
fireplaces 42-3, 78, 109
fixtures 11-26
flagstones 61
floors 45-64
  baseboards 31
  carpets 62-3
  doormats 102-3
  insulation 24
  laminated flooring
    54-5
  laying a subfloor 50-1
  leveling 57
  painting 52-3
  repairing 98-9
  sanding 46-7
  staining and varnishing
    48-9
  tiling 56-61
  vinyl 64
framing 36, 90-1

G
gas fireplaces 43, 110
glass 109
  doors 38
gripper rods 62, 86
grout 61, 96, 97

H
handles, doors 12-13
hardboard subfloors 50
hearths 42
hooks 88-9

I
insulation 24-5

K
kitchens 104-5

L
laminated finishes 54-5,
  109

leveling floors 57
lighting 92, 104
lipping 74
locks 16, 17

M
maintenance 110-11
marble tiles 61
mirrors 73, 84-5
mitered joints 30
moldings 40-1, 75, 76
mortise bolts 17

N
nails 31, 33

P
painting
  doors 38
  floors 52-3
  walls 106
paneling 32-3, 40-1
paper borders 91
parquet panels 59
particleboard subfloors
  51
peepholes 17
pegs 88
picture hanging 82-3
picture rails 28-9, 78
pipes, insulation 24, 25
plaster
  frames and roses 36-7
  textured plaster 44
plywood subfloors 51
poles, curtain 20-1

Q
quarry tiles 61

R
racks 70-1, 80
radiators 78, 109
rails, wooden 28-9
repairs, walls 94-5
roses, plaster 37

S
sanding floors 46-7
scribing 31
secret nailing 33
security fixtures 16-17,
  110
shelving 74-9
slate tiles 61
smoke alarms 26, 110
solid fuel fireplaces 43
sponged frames 90

staining floors 48-9
stairs, storage under
  66-7
stamping 74, 90, 96
stenciling 90, 96
stone tiles 61
storage 65-80
  ceiling systems 70-1
  cabinets 72-3
  shelving 74-9
  understairs 66-7
  window seats 68-9
subfloors 50-1, 53

T
textiles, hanging 86-7
textured plaster 44
throws, hanging 87
tiles 56-61, 96-7
tongue-and-groove 33,
  99
tools 9-10
tracks, curtain 18-19

U
understairs storage 66-7

V
valance, window 78
varnishing floors 48-9
viewers 17
vinyl flooring 64

W
wallpapering 107
walls
  baseboards 31
  insulation 24
  painting 106
  paneling 32-3
  papering 107
  repairing 94-5
  textured plaster 44
water supply 110, 111
wax, floors 49
windows
  double glazing 22-3
  insulation 24
  security fixtures 16
  shelving 79
  window furniture
    14-15, 109
  window seats 68-9
wood 108
wooden rails 28-9

All illustrations by Chris Forsey. All photographs by Tim Ridley except for the following pages:

l = left, r = right, c = centre, t = top, b = bottom

Page 5b Peter Reid/Houses & Interiors; 7t Camera Press, 7b Nick Huggins/Houses & Interiors; 8b Elizabeth Whiting & Associates; 22b Elizabeth Whiting & Associates; 23t Roger Brooks/Houses & Interiors; 38cl Elizabeth Whiting & Associates, 38cr Elizabeth Whiting & Associates; 38br Camera Press; 66l Camera Press; 67t Victor Watts/Houses & Interiors, 67b Elizabeth Whiting & Associates; 69b Simon Butcher/Houses & Interiors; 70c Peter Reid/Houses & Interiors, 70b Elizabeth Whiting & Associates; 72t Andrew Wood/The Interior Archive, 72c Camera Press, 72b Elizabeth Whiting & Associates; 92cr Nick Huggins/Houses & Interiors, 92cl Roger Brooks/Houses & Interiors, 92l Henry Wilson/The Interior Archive; 105b Elizabeth Whiting & Associates.